The
Attack on
Pearl Harbor

Thomas Streissguth, *Book Editor*

Daniel Leone, *Publisher*
Bonnie Szumski, *Editorial Director*
Scott Barbour, *Managing Editor*

OPPOSING
VIEWPOINTS®
SERIES

AT ISSUE IN HISTORY

Greenhaven Press, Inc.
San Diego, California

Library of Congress Cataloging-in-Publication Data

The attack on Pearl Harbor / Thomas Streissguth, book editor.
    p. cm.—(At issue in history)
    Includes bibliographical references and index.
    ISBN 0-7377-0752-6 (lib. bdg. : alk. paper)—
    ISBN 0-7377-0751-8 (pbk. : alk. paper)
    1. Pearl Harbor (Hawaii), Attack on, 1941. I. Streissguth, Thomas, 1958–   II. Series.

D767.92 .A79 2002
940.54'26—dc21

                                        2001042922

Cover photo: Library of Congress

© 2002 by Greenhaven Press, Inc., PO Box 289009, San Diego, CA 92198-9009

Printed in the U.S.A.

Contents

Chapter 3: The Pearl Harbor Debate

Foreword

Historian Robert Weiss defines history simply as "a record and interpretation of past events." Both elements—record and interpretation—are necessary, Weiss argues.

> Names, dates, places, and events are the essence of history. But historical writing is not a compendium of facts. It consists of facts placed in a sequence to tell a connected story. A work of history is not merely a story, however. It also must analyze what happened and *why*—that is, it must interpret the past for the reader.

For example, the events of December 7, 1941, that led President Franklin D. Roosevelt to call it "a date which will live in infamy" are fairly well known and straightforward. A force of Japanese planes and submarines launched a torpedo and bombing attack on American military targets in Pearl Harbor, Hawaii. The surprise assault sank five battleships, disabled or sank fourteen additional ships, and left almost twenty-four hundred American soldiers and sailors dead. On the following day, the United States formally entered World War II when Congress declared war on Japan.

These facts and consequences were almost immediately communicated to the American people who heard reports about Pearl Harbor and President Roosevelt's response on the radio. All realized that this was an important and pivotal event in American and world history. Yet the news from Pearl Harbor raised many unanswered questions. Why did Japan decide to launch such an offensive? Why were the attackers so successful in catching America by surprise? What did the attack reveal about the two nations, their people, and their leadership? What were its causes, and what were its effects? Political leaders, academic historians, and students look to learn the basic facts of historical events and to read the intepretations of these events by many different sources, both primary and secondary, in order to develop a more complete picture of the event in a historical context.

In the case of Pearl Harbor, several important questions surrounding the event remain in dispute, most notably the role of President Roosevelt. Some historians have blamed his policies for deliberately provoking Japan to attack in order to propel America into World War II; a few have gone so far as to accuse him of knowing of the impending attack but not informing others. Other historians, examining the same event, have exonerated the president of such charges, arguing that the historical evidence does not support such a theory.

The Greenhaven At Issue in History series recognizes that many important historical events have been interpreted differently and in some cases remain shrouded in controversy. Each volume features a collection of articles that focus on a topic that has sparked controversy among eyewitnesses, contemporary observers, and historians. An introductory essay sets the stage for each topic by presenting background and context. Several chapters then examine different facets of the subject at hand with readings chosen for their diversity of opinion. Each selection is preceded by a summary of the author's main points and conclusions. A bibliography is included for those students interested in pursuing further research. An annotated table of contents and thorough index help readers to quickly locate material of interest. Taken together, the contents of each of the volumes in the Greenhaven At Issue in History series will help students become more discriminating and thoughtful readers of history.

Introduction

The morning of December 7, 1941, began quietly in the Hawaiian Islands, a territory of the United States. A war was raging in Europe, Africa, and Asia, but the Western Hemisphere was still at peace. U.S. military ships and aircraft sat quietly at their stations in the harbors and airfields of Oahu, Hawaii's most populated island. The sunrise revealed a blue, clear sky over Oahu's Pearl Harbor, site of the principal U.S. naval base in the Pacific Ocean.

The peace would end at about ten minutes to eight that morning, as a wave of Japanese planes arrived from the north to carry out a surprise attack that would be the worst defeat ever suffered by the U.S. military. On the ground, confident navy and army commanders were caught completely unprepared. As bombs began falling on ships and planes, panicked young men scrambled desperately to load antiaircraft guns and get fighter planes into the air. Three waves of bombers, fighters, and torpedo planes swept over the island of Oahu, destroying or damaging 8 battleships, 9 other vessels, and 188 aircraft and killing or wounding about 3,500 military personnel and civilians. The president of the United States, Franklin Delano Roosevelt, would respond the next day by asking Congress for a declaration of war. But the damage had been done, and recovering from the attack on Pearl Harbor would take many months.

Background of the Attack

For several years prior to the Pearl Harbor attack, a militaristic regime in Japan had been extending its control to neighboring and distant nations in Asia. In 1937, the Japanese invaded China from the north. They attacked and destroyed American outposts and missions in China, and a gunboat, the *Panay*, was bombed and sunk in the Yangtze River on December 12, 1937. In 1939, the Japanese captured the port of Shanghai, a strategic European trading outpost in China. Japan took control of French Indochina in 1940, when France itself was conquered by Germany, and by December 1941, the Japanese army and navy were also threatening the Philippines and the Dutch East Indies (modern Indonesia). In the nations under its control, Japan had extended the "Greater East Asia Co-Prosperity Sphere," in which resources and manufacturing were dedicated to the rapid military buildup in the Japanese islands.

Germany invaded Poland on September 1, 1939, touching off World War II between Germany and Poland's allies Great Britain and France. The United States, under Roosevelt, remained neutral, although it was closely allied with the British. Believing that both Japan and Germany had to be stopped, Roosevelt first decided to try diplomatic action against the Japanese by denouncing a trade treaty the United States had made with Japan on July 26, 1939.

Many people in the United States opposed war with either Japan or Germany. The problems of Europe should remain European problems, in their opinion, and the United States should not get involved in Europe, fight for China, or protect colonies in Asia. American isolationism drew its strength from the memories of World War I and the desire to remain neutral rather than shedding blood for other countries. The isolationism played out against Roosevelt's insistence that the United States support its Allies to the fullest extend possible, short of actually fighting.

The U.S. government made its preparations for war. On June 14, 1940, Roosevelt signed a bill to increase military spending, which allowed the United States to begin construction of a two-ocean navy. In an attempt to build up a bipartisan effort for military preparedness, he appointed two Republicans to military cabinet positions: Henry Stimson as secretary of war and Frank Knox as secretary of the navy. In some locations, the country was already involved in a shooting war, as American merchant ships were sunk that fall after encounters with German U-boats. The neutral stance taken by the country's political and military leaders was all but forgotten by September 4, 1940, when Roosevelt ordered the navy to shoot any German submarines on sight.

Final Warnings

In the meantime, the nation's military intelligence agencies were intercepting and decoding telegraphic messages sent by the Japanese government to its diplomats abroad. Unknown to the Japanese, the United States had built several machines to automatically decrypt the "Magic" codes, used by the Japanese to communicate with their diplomats and admirals, as well as "Purple," the Magic code used for the most secret, urgent, and high-ranking diplomatic instructions. On all fronts, it seemed, the United States was ready for World War II.

In July 1941, Japan officially made Indochina a protectorate and a part of the Greater East Asia Co-Prosperity Sphere. Within Japan, a militant faction extended its control over the government. In October 1941, the cabinet of Prime Minister Prince Konoe fell. Konoe himself was replaced by the Japanese minister of war, Hideki Tojo. On November 20, 1941, Tojo sent an ultimatum to the United States: The United States must unfreeze Japanese assets, stop sending all military and economic aid to the Philippines, and stop aid to the Chinese leader Chiang Kai-shek, who was fighting Japan in China.

In the meantime, the leaders of the Japanese navy were giving the orders to carry out a long-planned surprise attack on the United States. On November 26, a force of 6 aircraft carriers with 423 airplanes, 2 battleships, 2 heavy cruisers, and 11 destroyers set out from the Kurile Islands, just north of Japan, into the North Pacific Ocean. On the next day, military leaders in Washington sent a "war warning" message to the Philippines and Pearl Harbor.

On December 6, perhaps hoping to avoid war, President Roosevelt made a final appeal to Japan's supreme leader, Emperor Hirohito. The appeal was ignored. That evening, a fourteen-part message was transmitted from Tokyo, the Japanese capital, to its embassies in the United States. The first thirteen parts were intercepted and passed to Roosevelt and to Cordell Hull, the secretary of state. On reading the message, Roosevelt turned to an assistant and observed: "This means war."

By this time, the president and his advisers were certain that Japan was preparing an attack, but they were not sure of the location. Most believed that it would be in the Philippines, the U.S. territory lying closest to Japan and its conquered territory in Asia. The Philippines, and the outpost of Guam, lying midway across the Pacific Ocean, formed the two outposts critical to any success the United States would have in challenging the Japanese in a Pacific Ocean war.

Tora, Tora, Tora!

On December 7, at 9:00 A.M., the final part of the 14-part message, in which Japan instructed its diplomats to break off diplomatic relations with the United States, was intercepted and decoded. The text of another message from Japan instructed the recipient to deliver this part of the message to the U.S. government at 1:00 P.M. Washington time—early morning in Pearl Harbor. The War Department sent out an alert, realizing that at 1:00 P.M. in Washington, dawn would be breaking in Hawaii, and conditions would be best for a surprise attack. But the warning was sent via Western Union, a commercial telegraph company, and did not arrive in Hawaii until the afternoon of December 7—several hours too late.

Before dawn in the Pacific Ocean, the Japanese striking force stopped 275 miles due north of Pearl Harbor and began launching the first wave of 183 planes. At 7:02, two radar operators at the Opana radar station on the northern shore of Oahu detected the first wave of incoming aircraft on their screens. The operators reported the images to their commanding officer, Lieutenant Kermit Taylor. It was the final warning of the coming battle. But Taylor instructed the men to disregard their radar, believing it to show a flight of U.S. B-17 bombers arriving as scheduled from the West Coast of the United States.

The first wave of Japanese dive-bombers, torpedo bombers, high-level bombers, and fighter planes arrived over Pearl Harbor at 7:53. Peering down from his lead plane, the commander of the attack, Mitsuo Fuchida, found the harbor and airfields quiet, unprepared. To the admirals waiting aboard the Japanese carriers, he relayed the prearranged signal: "Tora, Tora, Tora!" signifying that complete surprise had been achieved. The first wave swept over the ships at anchor, strafing and bombing, while dive bombers attacked military planes resting harmlessly on the tarmacs of nearby airfields.

The raid ended at 9:45. Eight U.S. battleships were damaged, 5 were sunk. Three light cruisers, 3 destroyers, and 3 other vessels were lost, as were 188 aircraft. The Japanese lost 27 planes as well as 5 midget submarines, which had attacked from the shallow waters within and just outside of Pearl Harbor. (Fortunately, 3 U.S. aircraft carriers—the *Enterprise*, the *Lexington*, and the *Saratoga*—happened to be

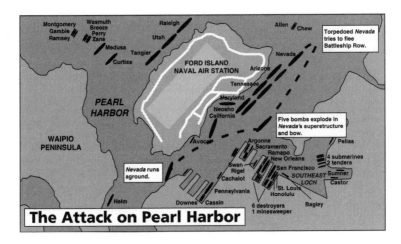

Montgomery
Gamble
Ramsey
Wasmuth
Breeze
Perry
Zane
Medusa
Tangier
Curtiss
Raleigh
Utah
Allen Chew
Nevada
FORD ISLAND
NAVAL AIR STATION
Arizona
Tennessee
Maryland
Neosho
California
Torpedoed *Nevada*
tries to flee
Battleship Row.
Five bombs explode in
Nevada's superstructure
and bow.
PEARL
HARBOR
WAIPIO
PENINSULA
Avocet
Argonne
Sacramento
Ramapo
New Orleans
San Francisco
Pelias
4 submarines
2 tenders
Nevada runs
aground.
Swan
Rigel
Cachalot
SOUTHEAST
LOCH
Sumner
Castor
St. Louis
Honolulu
Helm
Downes Cassin
Pennsylvania
6 destroyers
1 minesweeper
Bagley

The Attack on Pearl Harbor

out of port on maneuvers that morning.) By one estimate, a total of 2,335 military personnel and 68 civilians were killed in the attack; 1,178 were wounded. On the battleship *Arizona*, 1,104 men died when the ship settled to the bottom after a direct hit on its forward ammunition magazine.

At 2:30 P.M. Washington time, just after the attack on Pearl Harbor began, two Japanese diplomats delivered an official declaration of war to Secretary of State Cordell Hull.

On December 8, President Roosevelt appeared before a joint session of Congress and asked for a declaration of war on Japan. The declaration was readily given, and the United States entered World War II, approximately three months before a rapid preparation for a two-front war was to be completed by the army and navy. For three and a half years, the United States would fight this two-front war against Japan in Asia and Nazi Germany in Europe. Superior resources, training, and leadership would eventually overcome the early advantages brought by the surprise attacks by the Axis powers. The Allies overwhelmed Germany and captured its capital, Berlin, in the spring of 1945. In August, the United States exploded two atomic bombs over the Japanese cities of Hiroshima and Nagasaki. The Japanese surrendered, never having repeated the overwhelming and decisive victory they had achieved at Pearl Harbor.

Inquiries

Throughout the war, however, the humiliation of the Pearl Harbor defeat raised many questions. How could the United States, with its powerful military and its advanced intelligence agencies, be taken so completely by surprise? How could Admiral Husband Kimmel and Lieutenant General Walter Short, the military commanders at Pearl Harbor, have been so unprepared to defend their ships, planes, and bases in the face of an increasing military threat from Japan? How did the Japanese manage to conceal a large battle force north of Hawaii and halfway across the North Pacific Ocean? And how could the cabinet members and the president himself have not realized that Pearl Harbor presented such a ripe target for a surprise attack, which all agreed would be characteristic of Japanese military strategy?

Pearl Harbor turned out to be not only a military defeat, but also a military and political scandal. The questioning and investigations began almost immediately, and during World War II a total of eight official inquiries were held. The navy convened a Court of Inquiry, while the army organized the Pearl Harbor Board. The navy court directly criticized Admiral Harold Stark, chief of naval operations, for not advising Admiral Kimmel on the morning of the attack that Japan had broken off diplomatic relations with the United States. The army board blasted General Short for his unpreparedness and his lack of communication with naval commanders.

During the war, Admiral Kimmel and General Short were demoted and relieved of their commands; both resigned from the military under pressure. Dozens of staff officers were criticized for their inaction just before Pearl Harbor, as were George C. Marshall, army chief of staff, and Admiral Stark. The Naval Court of Inquiry and the Army Pearl Harbor Board also found fault with intelligence operations, with lower-ranking officers, with cabinet members, and with President Roosevelt.

Yet the case of Pearl Harbor did not close with the end of the war. During wartime, the need for secrecy—especially the need to keep Japan ignorant of the fact that its top-level codes had been broken—prevented a full-scale disclosure of the facts surrounding Pearl Harbor. After the war, several more official inquiries took place, while those who had been rebuked came forward with their own version of events. Admiral Kimmel mounted an energetic campaign to clear his name and posed some discomforting accusations against his commanders—including Admiral Stark and Roosevelt. Other naval officers revealed that they had been sworn to secrecy over the events leading up to Pearl Harbor and that sensitive documents, messages, and memoranda had disappeared from the offices of the military intelligence services. Books and articles appeared accusing both the army and navy of a whitewash. The Pearl Harbor attack took on a political tone as Republicans faulted a Democrat administration for incompetence and Democrats shot back accusations of partisan opportunism.

President Roosevelt's Role

In the aftermath of the war, one individual had escaped direct and official criticism: President Franklin Roosevelt. In the months after the president's death in April 1945, those investigating Pearl Harbor managed to keep a respectful silence about his role. But many unanswered questions about Roosevelt remained, and in the years since Pearl Harbor these questions turned into suspicions, then accusations. Several historians have concluded from the evidence and the sequence of events that the president deliberately provoked and fully expected a surprise attack from Japan.

These scholars claim that Roosevelt sought to join the Allies in World War II, but knew that Americans were sharply divided over participation in another foreign war. The bad memories of World War I had left the United States with a strong isolationist streak and a desire among many citizens to avoid getting involved yet again in the outside world's bloody wars and endless diplomatic conflicts. There seemed only one clear way to unite the country behind this purpose: a national sense of outrage and demand for vengeance against an enemy who carried out a treacherous surprise attack.

President Roosevelt had numerous defenders who found the Pearl Harbor conspiracy theory illogical and scandalous. They had several points to make. First and foremost, Roosevelt was a former secretary of the navy, a dedicated "navy man," and absolutely committed to the buildup of naval forces in the Pacific. He was a keen military strategist who realized that a war, and very possibly a two-front war, was coming, and soon. As such, it would have been absurd for the president to plot the destruction of his own forces. Second, even if Roosevelt was aware of a planned attack, and sought to bring the United States into the war, it would have been most logical for him to quietly forewarn his commanders so that damage to the fleet at Pearl Harbor could be contained. Finally, Roosevelt's defenders point out that Admiral Kimmel was indeed forewarned of a possible attack in the last week of November, when all Pacific commanders were sent a message that, in part, read: "This is a war warning. Execute an appropriate defensive deployment." The "war warning" message put full responsibility on Kimmel to ready his guns, ships, planes, and personnel for an imminent attack.

The answers to Roosevelt's accusers have not silenced the debate. Books, articles, and Internet pages continue to appear, summoning evidence to support one side or the other. Many people feel that Admiral Kimmel and General Short were scapegoats. Others feel that Roosevelt makes a convenient target for blame that should be concentrated on the military and its incompetence. Fifty years after Pearl Harbor, the central questions about the attack on Pearl Harbor remain. These questions are the topic of the following chapters.

Chapter 1

The Day of the Attack

1

The Attack from the Japanese Perspective

Gordon W. Prange

In the first days of December 1941, an immense fleet of air-craft carriers, tankers and escort vessels made its way across the choppy waters of the North Pacific Ocean. The Combined Fleet headquarters of the Imperial Japanese Navy had ordered the fleet to rendezvous at coordinates lying about 200 miles due north of the island of Oahu, in the U.S. Territory of Hawaii. From that point, an elaborate attack would be launched just before dawn on December 7, 1941. There had been no declaration of war between Japan and the United States; the two nations were still at peace.

The fleet was to maintain radio silence, avoid all contact with merchant shipping, and do its utmost to achieve surprise. Before reaching their destination, the pilots of the attacking force spent their waking hours in a study of maps and mock-ups of their targets: the ships of the U.S. Pacific Fleet as well as aircraft belonging to the American navy, army, and marines. For these pilots, the attack was the culmination of months of planning and training and a supreme test of their ability and bravery.

The following selection is excerpted from *God's Samurai*, historian Gordon W. Prange's biography of Mitsuo Fuchida, the air commander of the Pearl Harbor attack. Prange evokes the tension and excitement felt by the Japanese pilots and their sense of triumph on achieving the crucial element of surprise over the mighty military of the United States.

O n the voyage to Hawaii, Fuchida found plenty to oc-cupy his mind. He kept his airmen busy studying mock-ups of Pearl Harbor and Oahu, along with models of American warships, going over every angle of the tactics again and again until each man's part became second nature to him. The ships, though they maintained radio silence, received daily intelligence data relayed by Tokyo from the consulate on Oahu. [Vice Admiral Chiuchi] Nagumo fretted over the possibility that American submarines might be stalking the task force. Fuchida worried lest the admiral's attitude dampen morale. But, off duty, the airmen played games and drank sake or beer as if on a routine training mission.

The long-awaited message from Combined Fleet headquarters told the Nagumo force that Japan had decided the war would begin on 8 December 1941 Japanese time. In a way, the news came as a relief. Had Tokyo and Washington effected a reconciliation at the last minute, the letdown would almost have been unbearable.

The nearer they sailed to their objective, the warmer the weather grew. Officers and men shed winter clothing and took to shorts and shirts, spending as much time as possible above decks enjoying the fresh salt air. The sun shone only rarely. "The weather and the condition of the seas were so obviously in our favor that most of the officers considered it a special dispensation of providence," [Mineru] Genda remembered. The spiritually oriented [Ryunosuke] Kusaka repeated frequently, "This is the hand of God." Even Nagumo observed more than once, "When men work as hard as we have on this operation, Providence will favor them with its blessing."

Half the crews stood at battle alert. The chances of discovery increased with every plunge of the bows toward Hawaii. Fuchida moved among his airmen, distributing words of encouragement, answering questions, intervening with a smile at the slightest hint of disagreement or pessimism. [Shigeharu] Murata seconded his efforts with alacrity and kept everyone laughing.

The task force began refueling for the last time before the attack at 0830 on Saturday 6 December (local time). These were the most dangerous hours of the voyage, with the ships cruising at reduced speed far into enemy waters. So Nagumo ordered an all-out alert. When the last tanker steamed away for the postattack rendezvous point, the final link with home appeared to be severed.

But no one had time to brood. At 1130 the task force changed course to due south and increased speed to twenty knots. That night, after talking over various aspects of the attack for about an hour, the meeting of the staff and key airmen broke up in a mood of optimism, ready to accept whatever fate befell them. Nagumo and Kusaka stayed up most of the night in the operations room. Fuchida advised his flight leaders to get a good night's rest. Then he threw himself down on his bunk for a few hours. "I slept soundly," he recalled. "I had set up the whole machinery of the attack, and it was ready to go. There was no use worrying now."

The White Scarf

He jumped out of bed at about 0500 and pulled on his long red underwear, red shirt, and then his flying suit. Then he ate a quick but hearty breakfast. The *Akagi* pitched and tossed in the heavy seas. On a training maneuver Fuchida would not have permitted his pilots to take off. But this was a real operation, timed to the second. Throughout the Japanese empire the armed forces waited. Danger or no danger, they must get off the carriers.

On his way for a final report to Nagumo, Fuchida passed Genda in the gangway. For an instant they looked at one another. In that arrested moment, half a lifetime of understanding flashed between them. They smiled, and then Fuchida hurried to the flight deck for takeoff.

As Fuchida prepared to climb into his plane, the *Akagi*'s senior maintenance crewman handed him a white scarf. "All of the maintenance crew would like to go along to Pearl Harbor," he shouted above the roar of the engines. "Since we can't, we want you to take this *hachimaki* as a symbol that we are with you in spirit." Touched, Fuchida tied the scarf samurai-fashion around his flight helmet and scrambled into the aircraft.

Although the carriers bucked like broncos, takeoff met with surprisingly few mishaps. At about 0615 Fuchida signaled the circling aircraft to follow him south to the target. Even as his formation winged away, the mechanics were working frantically to bring the second wave of aircraft up to the flight decks. All told, the task force would launch 353 aircraft in this, the largest naval air armada ever sent aloft to that date.

As they flew toward Oahu, the first rays of dawn crept over the horizon. Then came the great red disk of the sun, looking like a huge Japanese naval flag. A chill of awe ran through Fuchida. He pushed back his canopy. The wind beat against his face and sent his *hachimaki* streaming out behind him like a banner. Behind him thundered the first attack wave, the rising sun glittering on its wings.

It was a glorious, inspiring sight. He was proud to be a man living at that time. The destiny of his country rested on his shoulders. O glorious dawn for Japan! he thought. Raising both arms, he waved exultantly to his air fleet. Some of the men saw the gesture and waved back.

Closing his canopy, he settled back to scan the sky for enemy aircraft. Clouds billowed below so thickly that he feared his pilot, Lieutenant Mutsuzaki, might overfly Oahu. He also worried about the weather obscuring the target. At that very instant, Honolulu radio obligingly gave his radioman a weather report indicating perfect visibility. This was followed with music to home in by. About 0730 Fuchida saw land below, all green foliage and white sands next to the sparking blue sea. "This is the north point of Oahu," he said to Mutsuzaki.

Fuchida could see no American patrol activity at sea or in the air, nor any sign of preparations for an attack.

As they flew on, Fuchida cried, "*Tenkai!*" indicating take attack position, and instructed Mutsuzaki to watch for enemy interceptors. So far, everything had worked out perfectly. By all the canons of the war gods, a snafu was long overdue. Fuchida could see no American patrol activity at sea or in the air, nor any sign of preparations for an attack.

Almost sure that the strike would come as a surprise, he fired a single Black Dragon rocket. Murata saw it and swung low toward the target. But Lieutenant Masaharu Suginami, a fighter-group leader, kept his aircraft in cruise position. Thinking he had missed the first rocket, Fuchida fired another. Then he groaned—[Kakuchi] Takahashi, mistaking the second rocket for the double signal meaning that the enemy was on the alert, swooped in with his dive-bombers. Fuchida ground his teeth in rage. Soon, however, he realized that the error made no practical difference.

Through his binoculars he looked at Pearl Harbor. What a majestic sight! There lay the beautiful harbor with all the great ships at anchor, so much like the model in Kusaka's cabin that it seemed unreal. Fuchida saw seven battleships, though according to the latest intelligence reports nine were in harbor. Undoubtedly someone had counted the old *Utah*, now a target ship. Fuchida didn't yet know that the flagship *Pennsylvania* was in dry dock. He was in no mood to quibble over a battlewagon or two. To his disappointment, there were no carriers in port. Preattack reports had indicated this, but he had hoped they were mistaken.

Deadly Fish

At 0749, somewhat off Lalalahi [Lualualei] Point, Fuchida grabbed the intercom and gave Mutsuzaki the attack signal: "*To! To! To!*" Then he ordered the radioman, First Flying Petty Officer Tokunobu Mizuki, to transmit the order to all pilots. The air fleet broke into its assigned parts. Fuchida's plane sped around Barbers Point. Certain now that they had caught the enemy unawares, Fuchida shouted, "*Tora! Tora! Tora!*" (Tiger! Tiger! Tiger!)—the code word signifying that they had achieved surprise.

For a fleeting moment, the tableau of the ships appeared fixed in time. Then events unwound at a furious pace. Suddenly the air was a confusing crisscross of planes as the first wave plunged down upon its targets. But no collisions marred the attacks. The men knew exactly what they were doing and went to work with ruthless precision.

[Shigeru] Itaya's Zeros [fighter planes] zoomed around like teams performing aerobatics, shooting up everything in sight. Takahashi's divebombers swooped down on Ford Island, exploding fires, erupting huge billows of smoke, loosing debris in every direction. At Battleship Row, Murata's torpedo bombers dropped so low it seemed they might tangle with the ships' superstructures. Fuchida was anxious about the torpedo attack, because the success of the plan depended heavily on it. He adjusted his binoculars, and the scene sharpened into focus. Murata and his men were splashing their deadly fish into the water, sending huge geysers shooting skyward.

Then Fuchida's own horizontal bombers swung over Battleship Row and he cried, "*Tsu! Tsu! Tsu!*" the order for them to go into action. Already antiaircraft bursts were dotting the sky. Fire came from the ships, and Fuchida felt a flicker of reluctant admiration. Just like Americans! he thought. If this were the Japanese fleet, it wouldn't have reacted so quickly. The Japanese are cut out for the offensive, not for the defensive.

At that moment, his plane quivered from a direct hit. Mutsuzaki assured him that everything was all right. No sooner had the words left his mouth than the plane rocked again, this time from a near miss. Reflecting on the need to overfly battleships at three thousand meters in the face of such fire, Fuchida wondered if his luck was not about to run out.

After three runs to ensure a good sighting, he dropped his bomb on the *California*, moored singly somewhat to the south of the double row. During his second run, he saw a terrible explosion. "The flame and smoke erupted skyward together," he recalled. "It was a hateful, mean-looking red flame, the kind that powder produces, and I knew at once that a big magazine had exploded." His plane shuddered in the suction of the after blast, but Mutsuzaki, skillful as he was brave, kept the damaged aircraft on an even keel.

Fuchida didn't know that he had witnessed the destruction of the *Arizona*; he only knew that at least one American battleship was out of action for good. Joy and gratification filled his heart; the mission would be a success.

Having dropped his single bomb, Fuchida fell back and exchanged places with his number-two aircraft. Henceforth his prime responsibility was to assess the damage for a report to Nagumo. Hovering out of range of antiaircraft flak, he looked down on a scene of desolation. The shattered hulk of the *Arizona* blazed like a forest fire, the *Oklahoma* had turned turtle, and the *California* and *West Virginia* were slowly settling. On the far side of Ford Island, the old *Utah* lay on her side, the victim of a mistake; the Japanese never intended to waste a precious torpedo on her. Across the channel near the navy yard and dry docks, the light cruiser *Helena* lay crippled.

Rolls of heavy smoke boiled up from Ford Island and Hickam and Wheeler Fields. Takahashi and Itaya had succeeded in pinning down Oahu's air power. The almost complete absence of American military aircraft in the skies told Fuchida that outlying airfields had suffered the same fate. The Japanese had complete control of the air over Oahu.

The Second Wave

At about 0840 Fuchida saw [Lt. Commander Shigekazu] Shimazaki's second wave thundering over the sea in perfect formation, on course and on schedule. Originally Fuchida had planned to take over the leadership of this wave, but soon he saw that Shimazaki was doing fine without his help. So he continued to observe the action and to record the damage.

Shimazaki's force did not include torpedo planes, which would have been highly vulnerable once the Japanese lost the vital element of surprise. This arrangement proved wise, for the second wave had a much rougher time than the first. Fuchida could see the muzzle flashes of antiaircraft guns belching black puffs of flak. From time to time, it chewed into the attacking planes and forced the pilots to maneuver out of its way. And a few American fighters buzzed into the second wave, doing well in view of the odds. Then there was the smoke rolling skyward from stricken ships and wrecked airfields, which made bombing difficult and hazardous.

Most of the power of the second wave rested in [Takeshiga] Egusa's capable hands. His men pounced on the *Nevada* as she tried to escape the deathtrap. This was the opportunity for which the Japanese longed—sinking a big ship in the narrow channel and bottling up Pearl Harbor. But the beleaguered *Nevada*, in spite of the blistering attack, crept down channel and beached near Hospital Point.

Behind the damaged *Pennsylvania*, in dry dock, Fuchida spotted two destroyers collapsed against one another like broken toys. Smoke seriously hampered his view. He hovered over the scene of destruction until certain that all his aircraft still skyborne had cleared the area. After making one final check of the damage, he instructed Mutsuzaki to go to the rendezvous point.

The men knew exactly what they were doing and went to work with ruthless precision.

In those days it was easy for a single-seated fighter plane to get lost on long overwater flights. Therefore, the Japanese had designated a rendezvous point for all aircraft off the northwest coast of Oahu, from which the bombers could guide the fighters to the carriers. There Fuchida's plane picked up a straggler or two and headed back toward the task force.

Remembering the grueling training he had put his men through, Fuchida's heart warmed. Those who attempted to accomplish the impossible had reaped their reward. And he felt a certain contempt for the U.S. Pacific Fleet. In a time of crisis threatening war, it had neglected to place antitorpedo nets around its battleships.

He was filled with pride of his men and of himself, and from his standpoint he had every right to be. The airmen had succeeded beyond all expectation. Years would pass, however, before Fuchida understood that he had left behind more than smashed ships and aircraft and dead and wounded men. He also left behind a nation welded together by the fires he and his men had set—a United States that would not rest until the Japanese had paid in full for their morning's work.

2

Eyewitness on Ford Island

Ted LeBaron

A member of Navy Patrol Squadron 22, Ted LeBaron witnessed the Pearl Harbor attack from his base on Ford Island, which lay in the center of Pearl Harbor. From the very first bombs dropping on nearby ships and airfields, to a glance at the bodies of the dead and wounded laying on the tables of a mess hall, the twenty-year-old LeBaron took in the many grim and terrifying images that are described in the following report.

Sunday morning was bright and clear and when I got up, I reached for my pants and as I started to put them on, noticed the time was 7:50. Where I was standing on the lanai [veranda] I was facing south which was the direction of our hangar. I could not see the hangar because of other intervening buildings but I knew the direction. At that moment I heard an explosion. When I looked up I could see a cloud of black smoke in the area of our hangar. I did not see the plane because it had apparently already climbed above the overhang of the floor above and was therefore out of my field of vision.

I have since had the feeling that I happened to be looking at the explosion of the first shot fired in anger at Pearl Harbor. I did see the second plane make his drop at the same location but I was looking at the rear of the plane straight on so no way to make any identification.

At this moment there was a commotion on the lanai on the opposite side of our wing. I ran the thirty or so feet over

From *Ted LeBaron on Ford Island*, by Ted LeBaron with Allan LeBaron, as found on the Pearl Harbor Remembered website at www.execpc.com/~dschaaf/lebaron.html.

to that side to see what the yelling was about. Looking up, but not very far up, I was looking at a Jap pilot in an open cockpit torpedo plane who was waving at us!

That first torpedo plane I saw had just finished his run on the *USS California*.

The next thing I was aware of, looking down Battleship Row at the other battleships, was that they were raising up out of the water a few feet and then settling back. Suddenly I realized that this action was being created by torpedoes. I think that the lifting of the outboard battleship was allowing another fish to get through to the inboard wagon to create this alternation of lifting and falling. It was right after this that we tried to get down to the hangar, but the order had come up that no one was to be allowed to leave the barracks.

I have since had the feeling that I happened to be looking at the explosion of the first shot fired in anger at Pearl Harbor.

This was a very bad time because all hell was breaking loose outside and we weren't even allowed to a position to see it. There was also some fear that the Japs might decide to bomb the barracks. This order held for only a few minutes, then we were allowed to get outside.

Up to this time which I imagine was about eight twenty or eight thirty, I remember pretty much the order of things. For the rest of the day I remember a lot of things but have not been able since to remember the order in which they happened.

Years ago I read "Day of Infamy" and the other day at the library, after I had started this, I thought of reading it then decided not to until I have finished putting down what I remember.

Running Aground

I have no idea how long it took me to get to the hangar. It involved going a few feet then ducking for cover either when I heard a lot of shrapnel or when a dive bomber would drop one on the *Nevada* which was then directly abreast of me. The *Nevada* was apparently on orders to get underway and leave the harbor, however I think the orders were changed when it was feared that it might be sunk in the harbor entrance and block the whole harbor. It was run aground at Hospital Point. As it moved up the harbor, the dive bombers were giving it a working over. They were not effective, to my knowledge.

Because of the death toll and the destruction at Pearl that day it is hard to imagine really exactly how safe I was even though I was right in the middle of the thing. First of all, after the first three or four bombs hit our hangar area, there were no bombs that were either aimed at or hit Ford Island. Because Ford Island was no longer a target the only risk was of being hit with shrapnel from antiaircraft fire. It has always been a source of amazement to me that more people were not victims of antiaircraft fallout that day. The most spectacular that day that I saw was when the destroyer *Shaw* blew up. Apparently a bomb got through to the magazines and it was blown apart.

I was directly across the channel from the dry dock when the *Shaw* blew and ran for cover expecting debris from that but none fell on Ford Island as far as I know. Sometime I heard the *Arizona* explosions but not in my view. When I did get to the hangar I think nearly all our planes were gutted from the burning of the gas in the wings. If any were salvageable, I don't remember.

Right as I arrived at the hangar one of the planes from the *Enterprise* was trying to land. Because of some itchy trigger fingers, the plane was being fired on by some of our men. I remember that the guy on duty in our hangar at the time of the bombing was firing his .45 at this plane. His name was Bill Bell and he was a bridge-playing pal of mine. He was a full-blooded Indian from Enid, Oklahoma—one of the most intense people I've ever met. He should have been dead but he wasn't, but he was one screaming Indian! I was yelling at him to stop, but at this point it's probably not surprising that he would have shot at anything with wings—he was maniacal about wanting to get even right then and completely frustrated by having only a .45 pistol, since all our machine guns had been destroyed by fire during the bombing.

The other reason for this firing which I don't think did any harm to the plane or the pilot. A group of us were running around yelling at guys who were firing from PBY's parked at an adjacent hangar. This firing can be understood when you realize that for the last hour or so, there was no danger of hitting any American planes since nothing but Jap planes had been in sight that morning. There was absolutely nothing to do at the hangar except stand around and look at each other. I remember Lt. Moorer calling a muster and making a speech about being at war and we were told to stay at the hangar and wait for orders.

The Ugliest Sight

Sometime later I went with a couple of other guys back to the barracks to get something to eat. The mess hall was on the first floor of our barracks and it was very large, covering most of the first floor. On this trip is when I saw the ugliest sight of the day. There had been many sailors who had either been blown into the water off the battleships or had jumped into the water to swim the short distance to Ford Island. The harbor was covered with oil from the torpedo hits and some drowned just trying to swim in the stuff. Some were wounded or burned before they entered the water. The mess hall was the natural place to take these men. When we entered the mess hall every single table had a man or a body stretched out on it. The eerie thing about it was that you could have heard a pin drop. I was more conscious of oil than I was of any blood in the scene. Some of these men were black with oil. I probably got something to eat but I don't remember it now.

The harbor was covered with oil from the torpedo hits and some drowned just trying to swim in the stuff.

On returning to the hangar it had become rumor time and there were some wild ones about invasions here and there, and the Japs coming back for another raid, etc.

Everyone was very uptight and the fact that there was nothing to do made it much worse. They came looking for some ordnance men volunteers to go to the utility hangars and service the *Enterprise* planes when and if they came in. We all jumped at it because at least it was something to do.

There was only one activity that had been going all day

and continued until dark and that was to fortify Ford Island. The main thing was to take every available machine gun out of any non-flyable planes and make machine gun nests on the edge of the island.

We didn't get any word through the day on when the *Enterprise* planes might be expected so we just waited. There were a couple of SBD dive bombers parked on the apron at the utility hangar and we spelled each other sitting in the rear cockpit to use that gun as antiaircraft if the need arose. During the evening, there were a couple of cases where there was some sporadic gunfire and in each case it would stop. We were speculating what would happen if everybody did open up at once but we were glad it didn't happen.

Another thing was the blackout. I have not seen one like that, before or since. It did not require any selling that it was necessary and it was complete, with armed sentries, passwords and the whole bit.

There was a water tower next to the runway which the carrier planes used and even the red light on that was blacked out.

Late that night we got the word that six of the *Enterprise* fighter planes would be coming in. The blackout would be maintained except that the red light on the water tower would be turned on. All the carrier pilots in the Pacific had at one time or another spent some time practicing night landings on Ford and would know where they were by using the light on the water tower as a locator. They were told to come in with their wingtip lights on but not to use their bright landing lights. They were probably told that everyone on the ground had been alerted so they would not get shot at.

A Tricky Landing

I don't know what went wrong but it was very bad! The planes made their approach from the southwest, which is the only approach since it was a single runway. At the last moment the lead pilot who may not have felt certain enough with only the water tower light to go by, decided not to land but to make another approach. He veered to the right and of course the others followed him. They were probably under one thousand feet at this time. Their new direction took them directly over what was left of the fleet.

Someone panicked and touched a trigger and every gun in that harbor opened up. Maybe there were some that didn't but it didn't seem that way. Just the tracers that went up that night furnished light of almost daylight intensity. We were standing by the two SBDs watching and swearing when we began to hear the sound of shrapnel hitting the runway. At this point no one said anything but we all turned and high-tailed it for cover. I found mine under a roof of concrete projecting over a loading platform at the rear of one of the hangars.

I thought that all six of those planes were dead ducks but in about ten minutes after all the guns were silent, two of the six came back and made the approach and landed. We ran out to the planes and one of them came tearing out of his cockpit yelling about what he thought of every blankety blank gunner in the U.S. fleet.

The other was frozen rigid and could not or would not move out of the cockpit for two or three minutes but was saying the same things. Surprisingly each plane had only two or three holes which did not affect its operation.

That was about it for the day of Pearl Harbor.

3

High-Level Chaos

Edwin T. Layton, with Roger Pineau, and John Costello

Lt. Commander Edwin T. Layton, Pacific Fleet Intelligence Officer, found himself at ground zero of the Japanese attack that came on the morning of December 7, and his anecdotal account of the events of that morning is one of the most vivid and complete pictures ever set down of the events at Pearl Harbor.

As Layton relates, the attack came as a complete surprise even to him—the man responsible for the most top secret information available to the fleet and its commander, Admiral Husband Kimmel. Layton does not assign, or accept, blame for the failure of military intelligence that made Pearl Harbor such a humiliating defeat. The following passage is reprinted from Layton's book *And I Was There*, which was completed by his collaborators, Captain Roger Pineau and historian John Costello, after Layton's death. Layton reveals that, despite the excellent facilities and skilled personnel in his department, nearly everyone responsible for intelligence matters at Pearl Harbor was one step behind the Japanese.

Unspotted by any American, the floatplane from the cruiser *Chikuma* winged its way north of Pearl Harbor and radioed back to the *Kido Butai*, "Enemy formation at anchor. Nine battleships, one heavy cruiser, six light cruisers are in harbor." This was followed by a detailed report of the wind and cloud conditions over the target. Simultaneously the *Toné*'s plane signaled from over Maui that there were no American warships in the Lahaina anchorage.

The report was relayed to [attack commander Mitsuo] Fuchida, whose plane was less than twenty-five miles north of

Oahu. He was straining through binoculars to penetrate the cloud breaks for a glimpse of the island's peaks. The Hawaiian radio station that had so accurately and unwittingly acted as his guide had just promised a warm, clear, sunny day when he was rewarded with his first sight of the terrain that had become so familiar from intense study of maps and photographs.

"All of a sudden the clouds broke, and a long line of coast appeared," Fuchida was to recall. "We were over Kahuku Point, the northern tip of the island, and it was now time for our deployment." Then came the only snag in the otherwise clockwork precision of the strike.

Fuchida, certain that one flight of torpedo bombers had not seen the flare he fired to send them in to attack an unalerted Pearl Harbor, fired another "Black Dragon." The wing leader of the dive bombers mistook the timing, and thought he had just witnessed the two-flare signal for a diversionary attack on Hickam Field and the naval strip at Ford Island. The dive bombers peeled away, climbed to twelve thousand feet, and came screaming down on our unsuspecting bases. Surprise was so complete that this hitch in the rehearsed precision of the raid was to make little difference.

"Notify all planes to attack," Fuchida ordered his radio operator.

The "TO, TO, TO" signal—an abbreviation for *totsugeki* ("charge")—was flashed out as Fuchida's bomber swung around Barbers Point. Seconds later, at 0753, the prearranged code signal, "TO RA, TO RA, TO RA," was tapped out over the airwaves. It was picked up over five thousand miles away by the aerials of the Combined Fleet flagship in the inland sea.

Admiral Yamamoto was engrossed in a round of *shogi* [Japanese chess] with his chief of staff. After receiving the message that complete surprise had been achieved, he continued clicking his counters across the hatched game board. The same traditional impassivity was not manifested by his pilots as they swept over the jewel-green checkerboard of Oahu's cane fields and pineapple plantations to rain destruction on the airstrips that were supposed to be the front line of Pearl Harbor's defense.

At Wheeler Field explosions and strafing runs tore apart the rows of parked fighters. On Ford Island bombs plastered the flying-boat slips, sending blazing chunks of PBYs roaring around like comets.

On Battleship Row

The torpedo bombers with their menacing instruments of destruction crowned by strange wooden boxes came looping in around Ford Island. Peeling off in pairs, they headed toward the line of battlewagons. The raid erupted with such sudden fury that it was vital minutes before those on board the helpless warships grasped what was happening.

Along Battleship Row the forenoon watch had just been piped to breakfast. Smartly drilled color parties were lined up on the fantails awaiting the bugler to signal the hour to break out ensigns. But the calls and the gentler sound of chiming chapel bells drifting across the harbor were abruptly drowned by the rattle of machine gun fire, the whistle of falling bombs, and the sickening crump of torpedo explosions.

The first "Kate" torpedo plane raced in so low over *Nevada* that it shredded the half-hoisted ensign with cannon fire. The sternmost battleship's astonished band continued to thump out a few more bars of "The Star-Spangled Banner" without missing a beat. Like a bloated steel lance the plane's torpedo splashed into the harbor abaft of *Arizona*, which was moored ahead. On board *Maryland* a seaman in the superstructure managed to break out a machine gun belt to open fire on two approaching torpedo planes.

The round of explosions that rocked Ford Island also roused the commander of the 2nd Patrol Wing. He broadcast an alarm from the control tower at 0758: "Air raid Pearl Harbor. This is not drill." Within a couple of minutes the shrill cry of alarm was taken up by the naval radio station, which began flashing it out to the United States.

The Kates attacked in tandem, and moments later torpedoes had slammed into *Oklahoma* and *West Virginia*. High aloft, Fuchida was encouraged by "tiny white flashes of smoke [and] wave rings in the water" as the assault concentrated on the outermost of the three pairs of battleships.

Kimmel was still in his dressing gown at just before 0800 when he took a call from the duty officer reporting that *Ward* had stopped a suspicious sampan. Murphy was still speaking when Kimmel's yeoman rushed in to tell him that the signal tower was broadcasting that the attack was no drill.

Kimmel had not yet finished buttoning his white jacket as he rushed outside. He stood transfixed for a few moments on the neighbors' lawn where he had a clear view of the planes circling over the harbor like angry hornets. "I knew right away that something terrible was going on," Kimmel would recall, "that this was not a casual raid by just a few stray planes."

I knew right away that something terrible was going on . . . that this was not a casual raid by just a few stray planes.

The first explosions rocked the underground headquarters of [navy cryptography] Station Hypo where Lieutenant Wesley "Ham" Wright was the duty officer that Sunday morning. The man he sent upstairs to check what was going on was Lieutenant John A. Williams, the only traffic analyst who had argued that the long radio silence of the Japanese carriers meant they were at sea. Williams must also have been the only man at Pearl Harbor that morning who was not surprised to see that the wheeling and diving planes had orange roundels on their wings. "They're Japanese aircraft and they're attacking Pearl Harbor," he came down to tell Wright in a flat voice.

My astonishment was complete when, at about the same time, my yeoman called me with the shocking news. At first I found it difficult to grasp, because the sight and sound of the fury erupting at Pearl Harbor was shut off from my house by the drop curtain of Diamond Head.

Minutes later my neighbor Lieutenant Paul Crosley picked me up in his Cadillac roadster. As we hurtled down into Honolulu, the nightmare grew larger the closer we came to the naval base, which radiated terrible explosions. I remember feeling that this was just a bad dream that could not be true.

Tall columns of smoke were rising from Battleship Row. Prompt flooding of the magazines had saved *West Virginia*. But in the first quarter hour a combined strike by bombs and torpedoes had caught the great battleship astern of her. *Arizona* erupted in a volcanic sheet of flame as her forward magazines ignited.

At the head of the row torpedoes had ripped open *Oklahoma*'s port side. She turned turtle within minutes, entombing more than four hundred crew members.

Waterspouts from bombs and torpedoes continued to burst skyward. Overhead the increasing number of black mushrooms of exploding antiaircraft shells were a hopeful indication that our gunners had recovered from their initial shock and were fighting back. Fuchida's plane was hit "as if struck by a huge club." A few holes and a severed control cable, however, did not stop the leader's [Mitsuo Fuchida's] bombing run over *Maryland*. Four missiles plummeted down to become "poppy seeds and finally disappeared just as two white flashes of smoke appeared on and near the ship."

Maryland was saved by her stoutly armored deck. Like *Tennessee* astern, her inboard position also protected her. While far from unscathed, the pair were the least damaged of all the battleships. Not so the battle force flagship. At her isolated forward berth *California* took two torpedoes and was settling by the head. *Nevada*, at the rear of Battleship Row, was struggling to get under way. She had cast off her moorings and every gun that could be trained aloft was firing at the dive bombers that swarmed down on her.

A little under half an hour after the attack began, its fury began to abate when the first wave of planes flew off. Across the harbor, destroyer *Helms* ran down and damaged another midget submarine, which would later beach and a single member of her two-man crew survive to surrender.

During the twenty-minute lull Admiral Kimmel reached his headquarters at the submarine base, while Crosley and I were still fighting our way through traffic with the help of a friendly motorcycle policeman. . . .

While Admiral [Claude] Bloch was telephoning an eyewitness account of the raid to the secretary of the navy, the second wave of the Japanese attack came winging in over Honolulu.

"He could look through a window," as Knox was to relate, "and see smoke and flames from the ships still burning in the harbor."

The renewal of the raid's intensity coincided with the arrival of the first of the B-17s flying in from the west coast. Unarmed and down to their last gallons of fuel after the fourteen-hour flight, the pilots nonetheless managed to land their bombers by scattering to airfields all over the island.

A hot reception also greeted the eighteen Dauntless dive bombers that had flown off [U.S. aircraft carrier] *Enterprise* an hour earlier. One was shot down by our own gunfire, and four by Japanese Zeros.

Not a single navy pilot managed to get aloft as 140 Japanese dive bombers and high-level bombers swept in from the east. Battling fearful odds, a handful of army pursuit planes did climb off from Bellows Field to knock eleven enemy planes out of a sky that was now being punctuated by the puffs of antiaircraft fire.

Retaliation came too late to save the battleships. Kimmel stood by the window of his office at the submarine base, his jaw set in stony anguish. As he watched the disaster across the harbor unfold with terrible fury, a spent .50-caliber machine gun bullet crashed through the glass. It brushed the admiral before it clanged to the floor. It cut his white jacket and raised a welt on his chest.

"It would have been merciful had it killed me," Kimmel murmured to his communications officer, Commander Maurice "Germany" Curts.

Later that day the admiral would show me the bullet and explain that although the practice was to turn over all captured enemy matériel to fleet intelligence, he would like to keep it.

The second wave of the attack was reaching its peak when destroyer *Monoghan* managed to ram a single midget submarine that was coolly firing a torpedo at the tender *Curtiss*, which was moored in the middle loch. The Japanese dive bombers concentrated their efforts on *Nevada* as she crawled past the blazing wreckage of Battleship Row. Her defiance was gamely cheered on by the men waiting to be rescued from the overturned *Oklahoma*.

Some *Arizona* survivors were picked up and helped man *Nevada*'s guns as the defiant battlewagon continued to fight off her attackers. The tugs that hurried out to prevent the listing battleship from sinking and blocking the main channel somehow managed to beach it at Waipo Point. It was the tugs' fire pumps that fought the flames that were threatening to engulf the battleship after her own fire main was knocked out by a bomb.

Nevada's dash for safety drew the Japanese bombers away from *Pennsylvania*, which was helplessly chocked up in the Number 1 Dry Dock. One bomb did penetrate the flagship's boat deck. Another bomb blew the bows off destroyer *Shaw* which was sharing the dock with the battleship and destroyer *Cassin*. The dry dock was flooded to douse the flames, but the intense heat of the burning fuel oil ignited the magazines and torpedo stores of both thin-hulled destroyers.

Shock and Wonder

Ten minutes before this terrific explosion rocked the southern end of the harbor, which occurred just after 0900, Crosley and I roared up to Pacific Fleet headquarters across the loch from the dry dock. Under such terrible circumstances, with antiaircraft gunfire blasting up from the submarines, there was no satisfaction in being greeted as the "man we should have been listening to." I felt numb, and very sick.

Everyone was stunned. Even my yeoman, who was normally as steady as a rock, was jittery as he handed me the intelligence log.

The atmosphere was one of general shock and electric wonder about what was going to happen next. Everyone was stunned. Even my yeoman, who was normally as steady as a rock, was jittery as he handed me the intelligence log that he had been keeping. It detailed the progress of the attack and listed the ships hit so far, those that were sinking, and others that were asking for assistance. It made me feel physically ill just to read it.

Looking out of my window, it was even more horrible to see *Oklahoma* upside down and *Arizona* ablaze. Seaplanes were burning like torches on the ramp at Ford Island.

I knew that men were out there dying. Oil was burning on the water and the sky was a pall of black smoke. Such a terrible scene of destruction was impossible ever to forget. There was another pyre rising over the hill from the marine corps field at Ewa. My log said that Wheeler Field had been knocked out and most of its planes destroyed. Kaneohe naval air station on the west side of the island was out of commission and under attack.

Captain [Charles H.] McMorris arrived at 0900 and immediately asked to see me. When I entered his office down the corridor I found the chief of war plans with [Vincent] Murphy and other members of his staff. They all looked at me as though it was a court-martial.

"Well, Layton, if it's any satisfaction to you, we were wrong and you were right," McMorris declared.

Of course I had been saying for weeks that Japan was planning aggressive moves, but it had not been my prediction at any time that they would open hostilities with an attack on Pearl Harbor. "Sir," I said, "it is no satisfaction to me whatsoever."

The *Cassin* and *Downes* were exploding in the dry dock as this exchange took place. It made me feel terrible. I excused myself and left to return to my office.

Now that the whole of Battleship Row lay under a billowing black cloud and a big blaze was raging in the dry dock, the Japanese bombers turned their attention to the northern side of Ford Island. During the final phase of their raid they damaged three light cruisers and sank the old battlewagon *Utah*, which was serving as a target ship.

It was during this final round that Ham Wright telephoned me from Hypo to tell me that they had just gotten a direction-finder bearing on radio signals made by the Japanese force. It was a "bilateral," a two-way reading of either 363 degrees or 183 degrees—this could mean that the carriers we had been trying to locate for so long were either due north or due south of us.

I wanted to know why the seventy-five-foot antenna of our top-secret CKK-X direction finder concealed high on a jungled peak to the north of Pearl Harbor could not give us a more accurate fix. "We can't get in communication with them," Wright told me. It later turned out that our telephone lines to it were army circuits. They had pulled the plugs on us when the emergency began and had not given us any warning.

Dreadful Pressure

When I went down to the operations room plot to lay down the two bearings, Admiral Kimmel came in. He was white and shaken, but determined to find a way of hitting back without delay. He wanted to know where the Japanese force was, and became uncharacteristically testy when I could not tell him whether the enemy carrier force was north or south.

"Goddammit! We're under attack here, everybody knows we're under attack," the admiral erupted. "Here you are, the fleet intelligence officer, and you don't even know whether they're north or south. For Christ's sake!"

The world had exploded in his face and I could not blame the admiral. If he had known at that moment that Washington had withheld vital intelligence from him, I believe he would have had a stroke then and there. The battleships were burning, ships were exploding, men were dying—and he was the man responsible. He had received no warning and then I was unable to tell him where our tormentors were. It was too much to ask any man to remain calm under such dreadful pressure.

All through the morning we had been receiving confusing and conflicting intelligence. Some army units were reporting an invasion had begun. "Enemy troops landing on north shore. Blue overalls with red emblems" was one message we received. Another reported paratroops landing on Barbers Point. It later transpired that both false reports had been triggered by a mechanic in dungarees who had parachuted to safety after his seaplane had been shot down by the Japanese.

The confusion was awful and inexcusable—and I felt bad about it. We would have been able to resolve our dilemma over where the carriers were if only Fort Shafter had relayed us the bearings plotted by the Opana radar truck. But they did not. The only report in which I had any confidence was [Joseph J.] Rochefort's. He telephoned me briefly as the raid was in its dying moments to tell me that the *Akagi* was the flagship of the attacking force.

"How do you know it's *Akagi*?" I asked. Joe explained, "It's the same ham-fisted radio operator who uses his transmitting key as if he is kicking it with his foot." But it was not much help to Kimmel that morning to know that the *Akagi* was two hundred miles away if I could not tell him whether the Japanese were north or south.

Captain McMorris was of the opinion that the Japanese must have come from the mandates and were therefore to southward. If so, [Admiral William F.] Halsey's task force was within striking distance. Accordingly, at 1046 Kimmel radioed Task Force 8: "DF bearings indicate enemy carrier bearing 178 from Barbers Point."

Shortly afterward four army bombers managed to get off from Hickam Field to begin searching the waters south of Barbers Point. They discovered *Minneapolis* steaming in the fleet exercise area. Such was the confusion that the heavy cruiser's report, "No carriers in sight," became garbled in translation to "Two carriers in sight." That afternoon a PBY patrol returning from Midway mistakenly bombed a cruiser of Admiral Wilson Brown's task force, which was also south of Oahu.

Before we're through with 'em, the Japanese language will be spoken only in hell.

Yet despite Kimmel's anger and frustration in his impatience to hit back, our confused intelligence picture that sent Halsey off on a fruitless chase to the south undoubtedly saved his force from destruction by the vastly superior Japanese striking force. This was no comfort to the fleet's pugnacious fighting admiral who returned to a still-smoking Pearl Harbor the next day vowing, "Before we're through with 'em, the Japanese language will be spoken only in hell.". . .

The Final Toll

After the last Japanese bomber had flown off northward, Fuchida's damaged plane continued to circle high above Pearl Harbor photographing the carnage: "I counted four battleships definitely sunk and three severely damaged and extensive damage had also been inflicted upon other types of ships. The seaplane base at Ford Island was all in flames, as were the airfields, especially Wheeler Field."

The pyre of dense black smoke that snaked thousands of feet into the clear sky was an awesome symbol of Japan's tactical victory and our defeat. The acrid stench of destruction haunted us that morning, punctuated by sporadic explosions and the flickering fires of burning ships and blazing oil. Our attackers might have flown off, but the havoc they had wreaked continued to grow as the nightmare translated itself into statistical reality with the ever-lengthening lists of casualties and the bill of destruction.

The final death toll, including 68 civilians, was to reach 2,403—nearly half of them were lost in *Arizona*. All told, some 1,178 were wounded—many of them burn victims whose lives were saved by the doctors who waged a success-

ful battle against infected burns with the new antibiotic sul-
fanilamide.

The attack had cost the fleet eighteen operational warships. Four battleships and *Utah* had been sunk; four were
severely damaged and only two were locally repairable.
Three light cruisers, three destroyers, and three auxiliary
craft had been put out of action, sunk, or wrecked beyond
repair. The navy had lost thirteen fighters, twenty-one scout
bombers, and forty-six patrol planes in addition to *Enterprise's* four dive bombers. The army air force losses were
even more punishing: eighteen bombers—including four B-
17s—and fifty-nine fighters. In addition there was extensive
damage to airfields and installations.

The death and destruction did not end when the bombs
stopped falling. Thousands of our men spent the day battling the flames as small craft, captains' gigs, and admirals'
barges were pressed into service dodging the pools of burning oil to snatch fuel-blackened survivors from the water.
For two days rescue teams and divers waged an agonizing
struggle to cut their way into compartments where trapped
men could be heard tapping desperately until air ran out.
Only thirty-four out of the four hundred entombed in the
capsized *Oklahoma* could be extricated alive.

Around 1100 the commander and staff officers of the
battle force reported to Kimmel's headquarters. While I was
checking the operations plot, I saw a short, heavyset officer
with a vice admiral's shoulder flashes, still wearing a life
jacket, his whites spotted with fuel oil, his face blackened by
smoke and soot. His eyes were almost shut; he looked dazed
as he stared off into space, not saying a word.

It was Admiral [William] Pye, who had assured me, almost twenty-four hours earlier to the minute, that the
Japanese would not attack us because "we were too strong
and powerful."

Chapter 2

The Official Response

1
The Day of Infamy

Franklin Delano Roosevelt

On the day after the attack on Pearl Harbor, President Roosevelt appeared before a joint session of Congress to ask legislators for a declaration of war against Japan. It had been twenty-three years since the close of World War I, a conflict that left a majority of Americans strongly opposed to any further involvement in European diplomacy and conflicts. It would take a sudden and malicious action on the part of the Axis to goad the Americans into war—and Pearl Harbor proved to be just that action. Roosevelt knew that, overnight, the attack had rallied public opinion in the United States to favor war. He moved quickly to declare war, and the Congress enthusiastically followed his lead with only Representative Jeannette Rankin of Montana dissenting.

Yesterday, December 7, 1941—a date which will live in infamy—the United States of America was suddenly and deliberately attacked by naval and air forces of the Empire of Japan.

The United States was at peace with that Nation and, at the solicitation of Japan, was still in conversation with its Government and its Emperor looking toward the maintenance of peace in the Pacific. Indeed, one hour after Japanese air squadrons had commenced bombing in Oahu, the Japanese Ambassador to the United States and his colleague delivered to the Secretary of State a formal reply to a recent American message. While this reply stated that it seemed useless to continue the existing diplomatic negotiations, it contained no threat or hint of war or armed attack.

Franklin Delano Roosevelt, address to Congress, December 8, 1941.

It will be recorded that the distance of Hawaii from Japan makes it obvious that the attack was deliberately planned many days or even weeks ago. During the intervening time the Japanese Government had deliberately sought to deceive the United States by false statements and expressions of hope for continued peace.

The attack yesterday on the Hawaiian Islands has caused severe damage to American naval and military forces. Very many American lives have been lost. In addition American ships have been reported torpedoed on the high seas between San Francisco and Honolulu.

Yesterday the Japanese Government also launched an attack against Malaya.

Last night Japanese forces attacked Hong Kong.

Last night Japanese forces attacked Guam.

Last night Japanese forces attacked the Philippine Islands.

Last night the Japanese attacked Midway Island.

Japan has, therefore, undertaken a surprise offensive extending throughout the Pacific area. The facts of yesterday speak for themselves. The people of the United States have already formed their opinions and well understand the implications to the very life and safety of our Nation.

As Commander-in-Chief of the Army and Navy I have directed that all measures be taken for our defense.

Always will we remember the character of the onslaught against us.

No matter how long it may take us to overcome this premeditated invasion, the American people in their righteous might will win through to absolute victory.

I believe I interpret the will of the Congress and of the people when I assert that we will not only defend ourselves to the uttermost but will make very certain that this form of treachery shall never endanger us again.

Hostilities exist. There is no blinking at the fact that our people, our territory, and our interests are in grave danger.

With confidence in our armed forces—with the unbounded determination of our people—we will gain the inevitable triumph—so help us God.

I ask that the Congress declare that since the unprovoked and dastardly attack by Japan on Sunday, December seventh, a state of war has existed between the United States and the Japanese Empire.

2

The Secretary of the Navy's Report

Frank Knox

After the Pearl Harbor attack, President Roosevelt sent Secretary of the Navy Frank Knox to Pearl Harbor to survey the base and estimate the time needed for salvage operations and to repair damaged vessels. A war was on; Roosevelt realized that Japan had delivered a serious blow to American military power in the Pacific, and he was anxious to get an accurate picture of the situation. Secretary Knox returned to Washington with two reports: a public report and the one which follows, originally marked "Top Secret" and meant only for high-level members of the Roosevelt administration.

While the public report was purposefully vague about the damage in order to mislead the Japanese, the Top Secret report was much more detailed. After studying the Knox Report, Roosevelt realized that the Pearl Harbor story would have to be studied further. Soon thereafter he ordered the commission headed by Supreme Court Justice Owen Roberts to meet and make a complete investigation. The Roberts Commission findings would be made public and, until the congressional investigations that took place after the war, would be considered the government's official version of events at Pearl Harbor.

The Japanese air attack on the island of Oahu on December 7th was a complete surprise to both the Army and the Navy. Its initial success, which included almost all the damage done, was due to a lack of a state of readiness against such an air attack, by both branches of the service. This statement was made by me to both General Short and Admiral Kimmel, and

Excerpted from Frank Knox's classified report to the president as entered into the hearings before the U.S. Congress Joint Committee on the Pearl Harbor Attack, part 24, pages 1,749–56.

both agreed that it was entirely true. Neither Army or Navy commandants in Oahu regarded such an attack as at all likely, because of the danger which such a carrier-borne attack would confront in view of the preponderance of the American naval strength in Hawaiian waters. While the likelihood of an attack without warning by Japan was in the minds of both General Short and Admiral Kimmel, both felt certain that such an attack would take place nearer Japan's base of operations, that is, in the Far East. Neither Short nor Kimmel, at the time of the attack, had any knowledge of the plain intimations of some surprise move, made clear in Washington, through the interception of Japanese instructions to Nomura, in which a surprise move of some kind was clearly indicated by the insistence upon the precise time of Nomura's reply to Hull, at one o'clock on Sunday.

A general war warning had been sent out from the Navy Department on November 27th, to Admiral Kimmel. General Short told me that a message of warning sent from the War Department on Saturday night at midnight, before the attack, failed to reach him until four or five hours after the attack had been made.

Both the Army and the Navy command at Oahu had prepared careful estimates covering their idea of the most likely and most imminent danger. General Short repeated to me several times that he felt the most imminent danger to the Army was the danger of sabotage, because of the known presence of large numbers of alien Japanese in Honolulu. Acting on this assumption, he took every possible measure to protect against this danger. This included, unfortunately, bunching the planes on the various fields on the island, close together, so that they might be carefully guarded against possible subversive action by Japanese agents. This condition, known as "Sabotage Alert" had been assumed because sabotage was considered as the most imminent danger to be guarded against. This bunching of planes, of course, made the Japanese air attack more effective. There was, to a lesser degree, the same lack of dispersal of planes on Navy stations, and although the possibility of sabotage was not given the same prominence in naval minds, both arms of the service lost most of their planes on the ground in the initial attack by the enemy. There were no Army planes in the air at the time of the attack and no planes were warmed up in readiness to take the air.

The Navy regarded the principal danger from a Japanese strike without warning was a submarine attack, and consequently made all necessary provisions to cope with such an attack. As a matter of fact, a submarine attack did accompany the air attack and at least two Japanese submarines were sunk and a third one ran ashore and was captured. No losses were incurred by the fleet from submarine attack. One small two man submarine penetrated into the harbor, having followed a vessel through the net, but because it broached in the shallow water it was immediately discovered by the *Curtiss* and was attacked and destroyed through the efforts of that vessel and those of the destroyer *Monaghan*. This submarine fired her torpedoes which hit a shoal to the west of Ford Island.

The Navy took no specific measures of protection against an air attack.

The Navy took no specific measures of protection against an air attack, save only that the ships in the harbor were so dispersed as to provide a field of fire covering every approach from the air. The Navy morning patrol was sent out at dawn to the southward, where the commander-in-chief had reason to suspect an attack might come. This patrol consisted of ten patrol bombers who made no contacts with enemy craft. At least 90% of officers and enlisted personnel were aboard ship when the attack came. The condition of readiness aboard ship was described as "Condition Three", which meant that about one-half of the broadside and anti-aircraft guns were manned, and all of the anti-aircraft guns were supplied with ammunition and were in readiness.

The first intimation of enemy action came to the Navy shortly after seven a. m., when a destroyer in the harbor entrance radioed that she had contacted a submarine and had (they believed) successfully depth charged it. Thus an attempted attack by submarine preceded the air attack by approximately a half hour. Quite a number of similar incidents, involving reports of submarine contact, had occurred in the recent past and too great credit was not given the destroyer commander's report. Subsequent investigation proved the report to be correct. Admiral Bloch received the report and weighed in his mind the possibility that it might be the start of action, but in view of submarine contacts in the past dismissed the thought.

The Army carried out no dawn patrol on Sunday, December 7th, the only air patrol being that sent to the southward by the Navy.

The radar equipment installed on shipboard is practically useless when the ships are in Pearl Harbor because of the surrounding mountains. Reliance therefore of both branches of the services is chiefly upon three Army detector stations on the island of Oahu. Until 7 December, it had been customary to operate three radars for a large portion of the day. However, on 6 December, permission was requested and obtained from the control officer to, on 7 December, operate only from 4:00 a.m. to 7:00 a.m. Accordingly, on 7 December, the stations were manned from before dawn until seven a. m., when they were closed officially. However, by pure chance one Army non-com officer remained at his post to practice on such planes as might take the air, and probably with no thought of enemy approach. At least a half hour before the attack was made this officer's radar indicator showed a concentration of planes to the northward, out 130 miles distant. He reported this to the Air Craft Warning Information Center, which was the place from which it should have been reported to headquarters. The officer there, a second lieutenant, took it upon his shoulders to pass it up, explaining that he had been told the *Enterprise* was at sea, and that the planes he had located were probably from that carrier. No report of this discovery of an enemy air force approaching from the north reached either the Army or the Navy commander. If this information had been properly handled, it would have given both Army and Navy sufficient warning to have been in a state of readiness, which at least would have prevented the major part of the damage done, and might easily have converted this successful air attack into a Japanese disaster.

The officer at the radar station, I was advised, showed this air force on his instrument as they came in and plotted their approach. I have seen the radar plot, which also included a plot of the enemy air forces returning to the carriers from which they had come to make the attack. This latter information did not reach the Navy until Tuesday, two days after the attack occurred, although many and varied reports as to various locations of radio bearings on the Japanese carriers did come to the Navy commander-in-chief.

The activities of Japanese fifth columnists [spies and saboteurs] immediately following the attack, took the form of spreading on the air by radio dozens of confusing and contradictory rumors concerning the direction in which the attacking planes had departed, as well as the presence in every direction of enemy ships. The Navy regarded the reports of concentration of enemy ships to the southward as most dependable and scouted at once in that direction. It is now believed that another unit of the Japanese force, using the call letters of their carriers, took station to the southward of Oahu and transmitted. Radio direction finder bearings on these transmittals aided in the false assumption that the enemy was to the southward. A force from the westward moved over from there in an attempt to intercept a Japanese force supposedly moving westward from a position south of Oahu. Subsequent information, based upon a chart recovered from a Japanese plane which was shot down, indicated that the Japanese forces actually retired to the northward. In any event, they were not contacted by either of the task forces, one of which was too far to the westward to have established contact on 7 December.

The Army anti-aircraft batteries were not manned when the attack was made and the mobile units were not in position. All Army personnel were in their quarters and the guns were not manned or in position for firing, save only those in fixed positions. Early anti-aircraft fire consisted almost exclusively of fire from .50 caliber machine guns.

The enemy attacked simultaneously on three Army fields, one Navy field and at Pearl Harbor. This attack was substantially unopposed except by very light and ineffective machine gun fire at the fields and stations. Generally speaking, the bombing attacks initially were directed at the air fields and the torpedo attacks at the ships in the harbor. The first return fire from the guns of the fleet began, it is estimated, about four minutes after the first torpedo was fired, and this fire grew rapidly in intensity.

Three waves of enemy air force swept over Pearl Harbor during the assault. As above stated, the first was substantially unopposed. The torpedo planes, flying low, appeared first over the hills surrounding the harbor, and in probably not more than sixty seconds were in a position to discharge their torpedoes. The second wave over the harbor was resisted with far greater fire power and a number of enemy planes were shot down. The third attack over the harbor was met by so intensive a barrage from the ships that it was driven off without getting the attack home, no effective hits being made in the harbor by this last assault.

The Army succeeded in getting ten fighter planes in the air before the enemy made the third and final sweep. And in the combat that ensued they estimate eleven enemy craft were shot down by plane or anti-aircraft fire. The Navy claims twelve more were destroyed by gunfire from the ships, making a total enemy loss of twenty-three. To these twenty-three, eighteen more may be added with reasonable assurances, these eighteen being Japanese planes which found themselves without sufficient fuel to return to their carriers and who plunged into the sea. Conversation between the planes and the Japanese fleet, in plain language, received in Oahu is the basis for this assumption. If true, it makes a total of forty-one planes lost by the Japanese.

The estimate of the number of planes attacking varies. This variance lies between a minimum of three carriers, carrying about fifty planes each, and a maximum of six carriers. This would indicate an attacking force somewhere between one hundred fifty and three hundred planes.

From the crashed Japanese planes considerable information was obtained concerning their general character. Papers discovered on a Japanese plane which crashed indicate a striking force of six carriers, three heavy cruisers and numerous auxiliary craft including destroyers and other vessels. It is interesting to note that the Japanese fighter planes were Model O-1, equipped with radial engines and built in early 1941. None of the planes shot down and so far examined, was fitted with any armored protection for the pilot nor were any self sealing gasoline tanks found in any plane. American radio and other American built equipment was recovered from the wreckage. One plane was armed with a Lewis gun of the 1920 vintage. Some observers believed that the planes carried an unusual number of rounds of ammunition and the use of explosive and incendiary 20 millimeter ammunition was a material factor in damaging planes and other objectives on the ground. The torpedo bombers were of an old type and used Whitehead torpedoes dating about 1906, equipped with large vanes on the stern to prevent the initial deep dive customary of torpedoes dropped by planes. It is pleasing to note that the attack has not disclosed any new or potent weapons. With this in mind, it was found that the armor piercing bombs employed were 15 [sic] inch A. P. projectiles, fitted with tail vanes.

In actual combat when American planes were able to take [to] the air, American fliers appear to have proved themselves considerably superior. One Army pilot alone is credited with shooting down four Japanese planes. All of the pilots who got in the air returned to the ground confident of their ability to handle Japanese air forces successfully in the future.

When American planes were able to take [to] the air, American fliers appear to have proved themselves considerably superior.

At neither Army or Navy air fields were planes dispersed. At Kaneohe [Naval Air Station] some VP planes were, however, moored in the water. They, too, were destroyed by machine gun fire, using incendiary bullets. Consequently, most of them were put out of action by the enemy in the initial sweep. Hangars on all of the fields were heavily bombed and many of them completely wrecked. At Hickam Field a very large barracks building was burned with heavy loss of life. The heaviest casualties in the Navy were incurred aboard ships subjected to torpedo attack. The bulk of the damage done to the fleet was done by torpedoes and not by bombs, some ships being hit by four or more torpedoes. With the sole exception of the *Arizona*, bombs proved ineffectual in causing serious damage.

Many of the officers and men of the crews when their ships were set afire were compelled to take to the water. A very considerable number were trapped below decks aboard the *Oklahoma* and the *Utah*, both of which capsized. By cutting through the bottom of these two vessels, while the attack was in progress, twenty six additional men were rescued alive. Throughout the action, small boats from other ships and from the harbor swarmed over the harbor engaged in the rescue of men who were driven overboard from their ships. The rescue of men from drowning and the recovery and swift treatment of the wounded was carried on throughout the engagement by both service people and civilians with the greatest gallantry.

Temporary hospital quarters were provided in half a dozen different places and the wounded were cared for promptly. Because of the huge number of unidentified dead, many being burned beyond recognition and a large number having been picked up in the harbor unrecognizable after several days in the water, several hundred were buried in a common grave on government land adjoining the Navy Yard. While I was still there bodies were being recovered from the water, but all were in a condition which prevented identification. Dispositions made by the commandant of the 14th Naval District (Admiral Bloch were adequate and were efficiently carried out.

Of the eight battleships in Pearl Harbor when the attack was made on 7 December, three escaped serious damage and can put to sea in a matter of a few days. These are the *Maryland*, *Pennsylvania*, and the *Tennessee*. The *Nevada* can be raised in a month, and will then require a complete overhaul. The *California* can be raised in two and one-half months, and then must be given temporary repairs in order to send her to the Pacific coast for a year's overhaul. The *West Virginia* can be raised in three months, and will require a year and a half to two years for overhaul. The *Oklahoma*, which was overturned, it is estimated, can be raised in four months. Whether she will be worth overhaul cannot be determined now. The *Arizona* is a total wreck, her forward magazine having exploded after she had been damaged by both torpedoes and bombs. The *Colorado* was on the Pacific coast for overhaul.

There were six cruisers in the harbor at the time of the attack. The *Detroit* put to sea at once and is uninjured. The *New Orleans* and the *San Francisco* are now ready to go to sea. The *Honolulu* will be ready on December 20th. The *Helena* was badly damaged and may require a new engine. She will be ready to go to the Pacific coast for overhaul December 31st. The *Raleigh* was flooded throughout her machinery spaces and seriously injured in other respects. It is estimated she will be ready for the trip to the Pacific coast for overhaul on January 15th.

There were ten destroyers in the harbor at the time of the attack. Seven of these put to sea at once and were uninjured. The *Cassin* and the *Downes* were in the same dry-dock with the *Pennsylvania*. Bombs designed for the *Pennsylvania* hit the two destroyers and totally wrecked both of them. Although both destroyers were badly burned prompt fire fighting work saved the *Pennsylvania* from any damage. The destroyer *Shaw* was in the floating dry-dock at the time of the attack. All of this ship forward of No. 1 stack was seriously damaged or blown off. The after-part of the ship is still intact and can be salvaged and a new section can be built to replace that part of the ship now destroyed.

The mine layer *Oglala* was lying moored outside the *Helena*, and received the impact of the torpedo attack designed for the cruiser. She is a total loss. The airplane tender *Curtiss* which was bombed and injured by fire started when a torpedo plane plunged into her crane will be ready for service on December 17th. The *Vestal*, one of the ships of the train which was damaged, will be ready to go to the Pacific coast on December 17th for overhaul. The old battleship *Utah*, which had been converted into a training ship for anti-aircraft instruction, is a total loss.

General Observations

There was no attempt by either Admiral Kimmel or General Short to alibi the lack of a state of readiness for the air attack. Both admitted they did not expect it and had taken no adequate measures to meet one if it came. Both Kimmel and Short evidently regarded an air attack as extremely unlikely because of the great distance which the Japs [sic] would have to travel to make the attack and the consequent exposure of such a task force to the superior gun power of the American fleet. Neither the Army nor the Navy commander expected that an attack would be made by the Japanese while negotiations were still proceeding in Washington. Both felt that if any surprise attack was attempted it would be made in the Far East.

Of course the best means of defense against air attack consists of fighter planes. Lack of an adequate number of this type of aircraft available to the Army for the defense of the island is due to the diversion of this type before the outbreak of the war, to the British, the Chinese, the Dutch and the Russians.

The next best weapon against air attack is adequate and well disposed anti-aircraft artillery. There is a dangerous shortage of guns of this type on the island. This is through no fault of the Army commander who has pressed consistently for these guns.

There was evident in both Army and Navy only a very slight feeling of apprehension of any attack at all and neither Army nor Navy were in a position of readiness because of this feeling.

It cannot be too strongly emphasized that there was available to the enemy in Oahu probably the most efficient fifth column to be found anywhere in the American possessions, due to the presence of very large numbers of alien Japanese. The intelligence work done by this fifth column before the attack provided the Japanese Navy with exact knowledge of all necessary details to plan the attack. This included exact charts showing customary position of ships when in Pearl Harbor, exact location of all defenses, gun power and numerous other details. Papers captured from the Japanese submarine that ran ashore indicated that the exact position of nearly every ship in the harbor was known and charted and all the necessary data to facilitate a submarine attack was in Japanese possession. It is an interesting fact that the *Utah* at the time of the attack occupied a berth normally used by an aircraft carrier and she was sunk and is a total loss. The work of the fifth column artists in Hawaii has only been approached in this war by the success of a similar group in Norway.

There was evident in both Army and Navy only a very slight feeling of apprehension of any attack at all.

The fighting spirit of the crews aboard ship and ashore was superb. Gun crews remained at their station with their guns in action until they slid into the water from the *Oklahoma*'s deck or were driven overboard by fires on other ships. Men ashore manned every available small boat and carried on rescue work saving the lives of the men who were driven overboard while the heaviest fighting was going on. Some of the crew of the *Utah*, swept from the deck of the ship as she capsized, were rescued by destroyers leaving the harbor to engage in an attack on the enemy forces. Although clad only in their underclothes, they insisted on joining the crews of the destroyers which rescued them and went to sea.

The evacuation of the wounded and the rescue of men from drowning was carried on with such superb courage and efficiency as to excite universal admiration, and additional hospital accommodations were quickly provided so that the wounded could be cared for as rapidly as they were brought ashore.

The removal of the convalescent wounded to the mainland promptly is imperative. I recommend that the *Solace* should be loaded with these convalescent wounded at once and brought to the coast with or without escort.

The reported attempted landing on the west coast of Oahu, near Lualualei was an effort on the part of the Japanese fifth columnists to direct the efforts of the U. S. task forces at sea and to lure these forces into a submarine trap. Fortunately, this fact was realized before certain light forces under Rear Admiral [Milo] Draemel reached the vicinity of the reported landings. His ships were turned away just prior to the launching of a number of torpedoes by waiting submarines, which torpedoes were sighted by the vessels in Admiral Draemel's force.

The same quality of courage and resourcefulness was displayed by the Naval forces ashore as by the men aboard ship. This was likewise true of hundreds of civilian employees in the yard, who participated in the fire fighting and rescue work from the beginning of the attack.

It is of significance to note that throughout the entire engagement on 7 December, no enemy air plane dropped any bombs on the oil storage tanks in which huge quantities of oil are stored. This was one of many indications that appear to foreshadow a renewal of the Japanese attack, probably with landing forces, in the near future. Every effort to strengthen our air defenses, particularly in pursuit planes and anti-aircraft artillery is clearly indicated. This anticipation of a renewal of the attack is shared by both Army and Navy Officers in Hawaii. As a matter of fact, in the ranks of the men in both services it is hoped for. Both are grimly determined to avenge the treachery which cost the lives of so many of their comrades. Instead of dampening their spirits, the Japanese attack has awakened in them a stern spirit of revenge that would be an important factor in the successful resistance of any new enemy approach. . . .

Summary and Recommendations

In conclusion may I invite particular attention to the following points in my report and draw certain conclusions therefrom:

(1) Neither the Army or the Navy commandant in Oahu regarded an air attack on the Army air fields or the Navy stations as at all likely.

(2) The Army and Naval commands had received a general war warning on November 27th, but a special war

warning sent out by the War Department at midnight December 7th to the Army was not received until some hours after the attack on that date.

(3) Army preparations were primarily based on fear of sabotage while the Navy's were based on fear of submarine attack. Therefore, no adequate measures were taken by either service to guard against a surprise air attack.

(4) Radar equipment manned by the Army and usually operated for a longer period, was only operated from 4:00 a.m. to 7:00 a.m., on December 7th. This change was authorized by the control officer. Accurate information of the approach of a concentration of planes 130 miles to the northward relayed to the Aircraft Warning Information Center by an unofficial observer was not relayed beyond that office. Nor was other information from Army radar showing the retirement of enemy aircraft to their bases received as such by the Navy until two days after the attack.

(5) The first surprise attack, simultaneously on five principal objectives, caught them all completely unprepared. It was about four minutes before the first anti-aircraft fire by the Navy began, and as the Army aircraft batteries were not manned nor their mobile units in position it was some time before their anti-aircraft fire became effective.

(6) Most of the damage to Army fields and Navy stations occurred during the first attack, which concentrated on planes, airfields and capital ships.

(7) As anti-aircraft fire increased the second and third attacks resulted in successively less damage.

(8) The final results of the three attacks left the Army air fields and the Naval station very badly damaged and resulted in the practical immobilization of the majority of the Navy's battle fleet in the Pacific for months to come, the loss of 75% of the Army's air forces on the Islands, and the loss of an even larger percentage of the Navy's air force on Oahu.

(9) Once action was joined the courage, determination and resourcefulness of the armed services and of the civilian employees left nothing to be desired. Individually and collectively the bravery of the defense was superb. In single unit combat the American pursuit planes proved themselves superior to the Japanese and the American personnel in the air demonstrated distinct superiority over the Japanese.

(10) While the bulk of the damage done to Naval ships was the result of aerial torpedoes, the only battleship that

was completely destroyed was hit by bombs and not by torpedoes. Hangars of the type used on all four [air] stations are a serious menace and should be abandoned for use for storage purposes in possible attack areas.

(11) The loss of life and the number of wounded in this attack is a shocking result of unpreparedness. The handling of the dead and wounded has been prompt and efficient. The wounded should be evacuated to the mainland as soon as possible.

(12) The families of combatant forces should be evacuated to the mainland as soon as possible. Orders to this end are already in preparation.

(13) Salvage facilities and personnel are excellent and, as presently to be augmented, will be ample to meet the station's needs and will place the damaged vessels in repair berths in the shortest possible time.

(14) Repair facilities are adequate to promptly carry out such repairs as are to be made on this Naval station. Auxiliary repair facilities are under consideration to relieve the yard from small craft and to lessen the concentration of vessels at one harbor.

(15) In view of the attack and the serious damage inflicted by it, the usefulness and availability of the Naval station must be restudied. Its air defenses must be strengthened immediately by the despatch of as many fighter planes and anti-aircraft guns as can be assigned to it. Special defenses against aerial torpedoes, such as balloon barrages and deep floats to be moored alongside important combatant units must be developed. Pending these studies and the addition of satisfactory safeguards, no large concentration of naval vessels can be permitted at Pearl Harbor.

(16) This attack has emphasized the completeness of the naval and military information in the hands of the Japanese, the meticulous detail of their plans of attack, and their courage, ability and resourcefulness in executing and pressing home their operation. It should serve as a mighty incentive to our defense forces to spare no effort to achieve a final victory.

3

The Army Pearl Harbor Board: Apportioning Blame for Pearl Harbor

George Grunert, Henry D. Russell, and Walter H. Frank

By the late spring of 1944, the United States was on the offensive in the Pacific Ocean, while in Europe an invasion of northern France boded ill for the future of Nazi Germany, Japan's ally. To certain members of Congress, it seemed the time was right for a thorough inquiry into Pearl Harbor on the part of the U.S. Army. As a result, Congress commissioned an Army Board of Inquiry on June 13, 1944, to ascertain the facts relating to the attack and make the appropriate recommendations. The Board of Inquiry held hearings in Washington, D.C.; in San Francisco, California; and Hawaii, and heard a total of 151 witnesses.

What follows is the conclusion of the Army Board report, which was submitted to Congress on October 20, 1944. The board members elaborate on earlier official inquiries, spread the blame to higher levels in the army—particularly to Chief of Staff George C. Marshall—and find that General Walter C. Short had "failed in his duties." The Army Board made no recommendations. To most historians, the Board of Inquiry report lacked one very crucial element: information on the Japanese diplomatic messages that the United States had intercepted and which provide the critical information on who might have expected a surprise Japanese attack in early December 1941.

From the conclusion of the Army Board of Inquiry report to Congress, submitted by George Grunert, Henry D. Russell, and Walter H. Frank, October 20, 1944.

Explanations

As prelude to the citation of conclusions the following is pertinent:

1. SCOPE: Attention is called to the fact that the record developed by the investigation of this Board contains a great amount of evidence, both oral and documentary, relating to incidents and issues about which no conclusions are drawn. Evidence was introduced on these so that anything which might have had a bearing on the Pearl Harbor disaster would be fully explored. The Board considered that its mission implied the revealing of all pertinent facts to the end that charges of concealment would be fully met. In formulating its conclusions the Board has selected for treatment only those things which it considers material for a clear understanding of the events which collectively caused the Pearl Harbor disaster. The full report of the Board discusses and analyses the testimony in its entirety and must be read for a clear understanding of the history of the Pearl Harbor attack.

2. ESTIMATES UPON WHICH ACTION WAS BASED: The responsible officers in the War Department and in the Hawaiian Department, without exception, so far as this Board has been able to determine, estimated by facts which then seemed to impel the conclusion that initially the impending war would be confined to the land and seas lying south of the Japanese homeland, as forces of the Japanese Army and Navy were concentrating and moving in that direction. British and Dutch forces were being organized and made ready to move in opposition. The Philippine Islands which were in this theater constituted a threat to the flank of the Japanese force if the United States should enter the war. Supplies and reinforcements were being rushed to the Philippines. There was complete ignorance of the existence of the task force which attacked Pearl Harbor. Intelligence officers in high places made the estimate and reached the conclusions in the light of these known facts. They followed a sane line of reasoning. These statements are in explanation, not justification.

The estimate was in error. The procedure in arriving at it was faulty, because it emphasized Japanese probabilities to the exclusion of their capabilities. Nevertheless, the thinking of these officers was colored and dominated by this estimate and their acts were similarly influenced.

3. RELATIONSHIP OF COMMANDERS IN HAWAII: The relations between General Short and Admiral [Husband E.] Kimmel and Admiral [Claude] Bloch, the commanders of the Army and Navy forces in Hawaii, were very cordial. They were making earnest and honest efforts to implement the plans which would result in the two services operating as a unit in an emergency. These highly desirable ends had not been accomplished at the time of the Pearl Harbor attack.

4. INTERCHANGE OF INFORMATION—STATE AND WAR DEPARTMENT: The Board was impressed with the apparent complete interchange of information between the State Department and the War Department. As a result the War Department was kept in close touch with international developments and the State Department knew of the Army's progress and its preparations for war.

Conclusions

a. The attack on the Territory of Hawaii was a surprise to all concerned: the nation, the War Department, and the Hawaiian Department. It was daring, well-conceived and well-executed, and it caught the defending forces practically unprepared to meet it or to minimize its destructiveness.

The attack on the Territory of Hawaii . . . was daring, well-conceived and well-executed, and it caught the defending forces practically unprepared.

---

b. The extent of the Pearl Harbor disaster was due primarily to two causes:

1. The failure of the Commanding General of the Hawaiian Department [General Short] adequately to alert his command for war, and

2. The failure of the War Department, with knowledge of the type of alert taken by the Commanding General, Hawaiian Department, to direct him to take an adequate alert, and the failure to keep him adequately informed as the developments of the United States–Japanese negotiations,

which in turn might have caused him to change from the inadequate alert to an adequate one.

c. We turn now to responsibilities:

1. The Secretary of State—the Honorable Cordell Hull. The action of the Secretary of State in delivering the counter-proposals of November 26, 1941, was used by the Japanese as the signal to begin the war by the attack on Pearl Harbor. To the extent that it hastened such attack it was in conflict with the efforts of the War and Navy Department to gain time for preparations for war. However, war with Japan was inevitable and imminent because of irreconcilable disagreements between the Japanese Empire and the American Government.

2. The Chief of Staff of the Army, General George C. Marshall, failed in his relations with the Hawaiian Department in the following particulars:

General George C. Marshall failed in his relations with the Hawaiian Department.

(a) To keep the Commanding General of the Hawaiian Department fully advised of the growing tenseness of the Japanese situation which indicated an increasing necessity for better preparation for war, of which information he had an abundance and [General] Short had little.

(b) To send additional instructions to the Commanding General of the Hawaiian Department on November 28, 1941, when evidently he failed to realize the import of General Short's reply of November 27th, which indicated clearly that General Short had misunderstood and misconstrued the ["War Warning"] message of November 27 and had not adequately alerted his command for war.

(c) To get to General Short on the evening of December 6th and the early morning of December 7th, the critical information indicating an almost immediate break with Japan, though there was ample time to have accomplished this.

(d) To investigate and determine the state of readiness of the Hawaiian Command between November 27 and December 7, 1941, despite the impending threat of war.

3. Chief of the War Plans Division, War Department

General Staff, Major General Leonard T. Gerow, failed in his duties in the following particulars:

(a) To keep the Commanding General, Hawaiian Department, adequately informed on the impending war situation by making available to him the substance of the data being delivered to the War Plans Division by the Assistant Chief of Staff, G-2.

(b) To send to the Commanding General of the Hawaiian Department on November 27, 1941, a clear, concise directive; on the contrary he approved the message of November 27, 1941, which contained confusing statements.

(c) To realize that the state of readiness reported in [General] Short's reply to the November 27th message was not a state of readiness for war, and he failed to take corrective action.

(d) To take the required steps to implement the existing joint plans and agreements between the Army and Navy to insure the functioning of the two services in the manner contemplated.

4. Commanding General of the Hawaiian Department, Lieutenant General Walter C. Short, failed in his duties in the following particulars:

(a) To place his command in a state of readiness for war in the face of a war warning by adopting an alert against sabotage only. The information which he had was incomplete and confusing but it was sufficient to warn him of the tense relations between our government and the Japanese Empire and that hostilities might be momentarily expected. This required that he guard against surprise to the extent possible and make ready his command so that it might be employed to the maximum and in time against the worst form of attack that the enemy might launch.

(b) To reach or attempt to reach an agreement with the Admiral commanding the Pacific Fleet [Admiral Kimmel] and the Admiral commanding the 14th Naval District [Admiral Bloch] for implementing the joint Army and Navy plans and agreements then in existence which provided for joint action by the two services. One of the methods by which they might have become operative was through the joint agreement of the responsible commanders.

(c) To inform himself of the effectiveness of the long-distance reconnaissance being conducted by the Navy.

(d) To replace inefficient staff officers.

Recommendations

Recommendations: NONE
George Grunert
Lieut. General, U.S. Army.
President
Henry D. Russell
Major General, U.S. Army.
Member.

Walter H. Frank
Major General, U.S. Army.
Member.

Friday,
20 October 1944.

4

The Dorn Report

Edwin Dorn

The questions surrounding Pearl Harbor did not cease with the official military and congressional investigations of the attack. Historians kept the debate over Pearl Harbor alive in their many books and articles, while military men rehashed the blame for unpreparedness at the highest levels. The families of Admiral Husband E. Kimmel and General Walter C. Short, in particular, wanted to restore the reputations of two men whom they believed had been unfairly blamed. They demanded that the subject stay in the public eye, and that the government keep looking into the official and unofficial actions at the highest levels of the Roosevelt administration. Their goal was the posthumous reinstatement of Admiral Kimmel and General Short to the four-star and three-star rank they had held, respectively, before the attack.

This pressure led to a request by Senator Strom Thurmond of South Carolina for another investigation, which would be carried out by Undersecretary of Defense Edwin Dorn. The Dorn Report, released in December 1995, found that Kimmel and Short had unfairly shouldered the burden of blame for Pearl Harbor. But Dorn also concluded that the two Pearl Harbor leaders were not victims of unfair official actions, and thus there could be "no official remedy" for Kimmel and Short or their families.

MEMORANDUM FOR THE DEPUTY SECRETARY OF DEFENSE

SUBJECT: Advancement of Rear Admiral Kimmel and Major General Short

This review was undertaken in response to a commitment that former Deputy Secretary [of Defense John]

From Edwin Dorn, memorandum to the deputy secretary of defense, December 15, 1995.

Deutch made to Senator Thurmond in April 1995. You assigned me to conduct it. In essence, you asked me to advise you whether actions taken toward General Short and Admiral Kimmel some 50 years ago were excessively harsh, and if so, whether posthumous advancement to three- and four-star rank is the appropriate remedy.

These issues are immediate and highly emotional to the descendants of Admiral Kimmel and General Short. Family members feel that the Pearl Harbor commanders were scapegoats for a disaster that they could neither prevent nor mitigate, and that others who were blameworthy escaped both official censure and public humiliation. They argue that advancement (or, as they put it, restoration to highest rank held) is the best way to remove the stigma and obloquy.

More is at stake here than the reputations of two officers and the feelings of their families. The principle of equity requires that wrongs be set right. In addition, we owe it to posterity to ensure that our history is told correctly. With support from a small team of [Defense Department] civilians and military officers, I studied the performance of the two commanders, the procedures that led to their relief and retirement and the reports of the several Pearl Harbor investigations. I also tried to understand the basis for the families' claim that General Short and Admiral Kimmel were unfairly denied restoration to three-star and four-star rank when that action became legally possible in 1947. The team reviewed thousands of pages of documents, read a number of secondary sources, visited Pearl Harbor and interviewed members of the families.

My findings are:

1. Responsibility for the Pearl Harbor disaster should not fall solely on the shoulders of Admiral Kimmel and General Short; it should be broadly shared.

a. The United States and Japan were pursuing policies that were leading inexorably to war. Japan had occupied Manchuria, was threatening much of Asia and had joined in a tripartite alliance with Italy and Germany. The US reaction was to stop selling Japan strategically important materials including oil (Japan bought most of its oil from the US) and, in the summer of 1941, to freeze Japanese assets in the US. Negotiations in the summer and fall of 1941 failed to break the impasse. By late November 1941, civilian and military leaders in the US had concluded that conflict was imminent; the only questions were when and where it would occur.

b. Admiral Kimmel and General Short were both sent "war warning" messages on November 27. They were advised that negotiations were stalemated and that Japan might take hostile action at any moment. Admiral Kimmel was ordered to execute a "defensive deployment" consistent with the US war plan in the Pacific; General Short was ordered to undertake "reconnaissance and other measures . . .", but his instructions were muddied somewhat by advice to avoid actions that would "alarm [Hawaii's] civil population or disclose intent."

Admiral Kimmel and General Short were both sent "war warning" messages on November 27.

---

c. Admiral Kimmel and General Short discussed the November 27 war warning, but concluded that an attack would occur in the Western Pacific, not in Hawaii. Indeed, the November 27 messages had mentioned the likelihood that the attack would occur in "the Philippines, Thai or Kra Peninsula or . . . Borneo." Washington also did not expect Hawaii to be attacked. Further, it appears that Admiral Kimmel and General Short were depending on timely tactical warning from Washington, should Hawaii become a target. Military leaders in Washington, on the other hand, appear to have felt that the November 27 war warning would lead Admiral Kimmel and General Short to heighten their vigilance, and failed to examine closely what they actually were doing.

d. Officials in Washington did not send Admiral Kimmel and General Short other information, derived from the Magic project that broke the Japanese code, that might have given them a greater sense of urgency and caused them to surmise that Hawaii was a likely target. For example, Washington did not tell them that Japanese agents in Hawaii had been instructed to report on the precise location of ships at Pearl Harbor. (The Japanese attacked Hawaii, the Philippines and several other targets on the same day.)

e. Information-sharing and operational cooperation

were hampered by bureaucratic rivalries. The Army and Navy were separate executive departments reporting directly to the President, and only the President could ensure that they were working together. Admiral Kimmel and General Short had cordial personal relations, but felt it inappropriate to inquire into one another's professional domains. This apparently was the standard at the time. General Short's mission was to defend the fleet in Hawaii; Admiral Kimmel apparently never asked in detail about General Short's plans. Admiral Kimmel's mission was to prepare for offensive operations against Japan. Early in 1941 the Navy also had assumed from the Army responsibility for conducting long-range aerial reconnaissance. Even after receiving the war warning, General Short apparently did not ask Admiral Kimmel whether the Navy actually was conducting long-range air patrols. Nevertheless, General Short assumed that he would receive the advance warning needed to launch Army Air Corps fighters, which were on four-hour alert, and to ready his antiaircraft guns, whose ammunition was stored some distance from the batteries. Just as Washington did not provide the Hawaii commanders with all the intelligence that was derived from Magic, so it also appears that Admiral Kimmel had more intelligence than he chose to share with General Short. For example, Admiral Kimmel learned on December 2 that several Japanese carriers were "lost" to US intelligence; their radio signals had not been detected for more than two weeks. He did not tell General Short.

The run-up to Pearl Harbor was fraught with miscommunication, oversights and lack of follow-up.

---

f. The run-up to Pearl Harbor was fraught with miscommunication, oversights and lack of follow-up. In his November 27 war warning message, Army Chief of Staff Marshall directed General Short to "undertake such reconnaissance and other measures as you deem necessary . . ." General Short assumed this order was misworded, because he believed General Marshall knew that the Navy had taken over the reconnaissance responsibility from the Army. He also assumed that the Navy was doing it. General Short's response to General Marshall described plans to defend against sabotage, but said nothing about reconnaissance. Apparently, no one in the War Department took note of the omission. The November 27 war warning from Admiral Stark, the Chief of Naval Operations (CNO), instructed Admiral Kimmel to undertake a "defensive deployment preparatory to carrying out the tasks assigned in WPL 46; [the war plan]." Exactly what Admiral Stark intended is not clear. Admiral Kimmel interpreted the CNO's guidance to mean that he (Admiral Kimmel) should continue what he had been doing for several weeks—sending submarines and planes to patrol around Wake and Midway, and patrolling outside Pearl Harbor for Japanese submarines. Carrier task forces en route to Wake and Midway were doing aerial reconnaissance as part of their normal training, thus covering a portion of the Pacific west and southwest of Hawaii. "Deployment" also could have meant to sortie the fleet from Pearl Harbor. Admiral Kimmel did not do that. Instead, he kept his ships in port, but pointed their bows toward the entrance so that they could leave quickly if the need arose. Moving several dozen warships through Pearl Harbor's narrow channel and into fighting posture on the high seas would have taken several hours. No one in the Department of Navy took issue with Admiral Kimmel's interpretation of the CNO's instructions.

g. Resources were scarce. Washington didn't have enough cryptologists and linguists to decode all the Japanese message traffic, so the analysts gave priority to diplomatic traffic over military traffic. The Navy in Hawaii was short of planes and crews. The Army in Hawaii was short of munitions.

h. Finally, the Japanese attack was brilliantly conceived and flawlessly executed. It involved a bold new use of carriers. It required crossing four thousand miles of ocean undetected, which meant taking the storm-tossed northern route where there was little commercial shipping. It required new technology—torpedoes that could be used in the shallow, narrow confines of Pearl Harbor. And the attack required extraordinarily well trained air crews with commanders capable of coordinating more than 150 planes in each wave of attack. US Naval exercises during the 1930s and the British Navy's 1940 raid on the Italian fleet at Taranto had demonstrated the feasibility of carrier-based attacks. But the scale and complexity of the Japanese attack greatly exceeded anything envisioned before. American military experts underestimated Japanese capability.

2. To say that responsibility is broadly shared is not to absolve Admiral Kimmel and General Short of accountability.

a. Military command is unique. A commander has plenary responsibility for the welfare of the people under his or her command, and is directly accountable for everything the unit does or fails to do. When a ship runs aground, the captain is accountable whether or not he/she was on the bridge at the time. When a unit is attacked, it is the commander and not the intelligence officer or the sentry who is accountable. Command at the three- and four-star level involves daunting responsibilities. Military officers at that level operate with a great deal of independence. They must have extraordinary skill, foresight and judgment, and a willingness to be accountable for things about which they could not possibly have personal knowledge. Today, for example, the senior commander in Hawaii is responsible for US military operations spanning half the world's surface—from the west coast of the United States to the east coast of Asia. His fleets sail the Pacific, the Indian Ocean, the China Sea, the Sea of Japan, the Arctic and the Antarctic. This, in the understated language of military law, is "a position of importance and responsibility."

b. It was appropriate that Admiral Kimmel and General Short be relieved. In the immediate aftermath of the attack, their relief was occasioned by the need to restore confidence in the Navy and Army's leadership, especially in the Pacific, and to get going with the war. Subsequently, investigations concluded that both commanders made errors of judgment. I have seen no information that leads me to contradict that conclusion.

c. The intelligence available to Admiral Kimmel and General Short was sufficient to justify a higher level of vigilance than they chose to maintain. They knew that war was imminent, they knew that Japanese tactics featured surprise attacks, and Admiral Kimmel (though not General Short) knew that the US had lost track of Japan's carriers. Further, they had the resources to maintain a higher level of vigilance. Admiral Kimmel believed that the optimum aerial reconnaissance would require covering 360 degrees around Hawaii for a sustained period. The Navy clearly did not have enough planes for that. This does not mean, however, that Admiral Kimmel had to choose between ideal aerial reconnaissance and no aerial reconnaissance. The fleet also had cruisers and destroyers that could have been used as pickets to supplement air patrols, but were not.

d. Different choices might not have discovered the carrier armada and might not have prevented the attack, but different choices—a different allocation of resources—could have reduced the magnitude of the disaster. The Navy and the Army were at a low level of alert against aerial attack. Shipboard anti-aircraft guns were firing within five minutes. The Army was not able to bring its batteries into play during the first wave of the attack and only four Army Air Corps fighters managed to get airborne. US losses included 2,403 dead (1,177 of whom are entombed in the *Arizona*), 1,178 wounded, eight battleships, ten other vessels and more than 100 aircraft. Japanese losses were 29 aircraft, one large submarine and five midget submarines.

3. The official treatment of Admiral Kimmel and General Short was substantively temperate and procedurally proper.

a. Admiral Kimmel and General Short were the objects of public vilification. At least one member of Congress demanded that they be summarily dismissed, stripped of rank and denied retirement benefits. They received hate mail and death threats. The public and Congress were clamoring for information about Pearl Harbor. The news media went into a feeding frenzy, gobbling up tidbits of blame and punishment. Under the circumstances, it is not surprising that information very hurtful to Admiral Kimmel and General Short—information implying that they would be court martialed, for example—was given to the press. These things happen, often not for the most honorable of reasons. This does not mean, however, that Admiral Kimmel and General Short were victims of a smear campaign orchestrated by government officials.

b. In contrast to their treatment by some of the media, their official treatment was substantively temperate. They were relieved, they reverted to two-star rank, and under the laws in force at the time, their retirements were at the two-star level. Although there was mention of court martial, no charges were brought. Indeed, official statements and investigations seemed purposely to avoid wording that would lead to court martial. For example, the Roberts Commission used the phrase "dereliction of duty"—a stinging rebuke, but at the time not a court martial offense. The Roberts Commission avoided other phrases, such as "culpable inefficiency" and "neglect of duty", that were court martial offenses. Later investigations such as the Joint Congressional Committee report eschewed "dereliction" in favor of "errors of judgment."

c. Admiral Kimmel requested a court martial in order to clear his name, but the request was not acted on. There is an allegation that the government feared bringing charges because a court martial would have put other senior military and civilian leaders in a bad light. This is possible. But it is equally possible that there simply were not sufficient grounds to sustain a successful prosecution. A court martial almost certainly would have revealed the existence of Magic, a key US intelligence asset.

d. I do not find major fault with the procedures used in the investigations. Family members have complained that Admiral Kimmel and General Short were denied "due process"; that is, they were not allowed to call their own witnesses or to cross-examine witnesses. But the calling and cross-examination of witnesses is characteristic of trials, not of investigations. Some of the investigations may have been more thorough than others, but I do not see a convincing basis for concluding that Admiral Kimmel and General Short were victims of government scapegoating or of a government-inspired smear campaign.

4. History has not been hostile to Admiral Kimmel and General Short.

a. None of the official reports ever held that Admiral Kimmel and General Short were solely responsible for the Pearl Harbor disaster, although the Roberts Commission came close. Later reports eschewed the stinging "dereliction of duty" rebuke in favor of "errors of judgment."

b. Historians who write about Pearl Harbor seem to be divided into three camps: those who hold Admiral Kimmel and General Short partly (but not solely) responsible; those who believe they were scapegoats; and those who lay much of the blame on bureaucratic factors such as the lack of coordination between the Army and the Navy. National Park

Service guides at the *Arizona* Memorial, for example, focus on the factors that led to war and on the tactics used in the attack, not on individual military leaders. A 30-minute film produced exclusively for use at the *Arizona* Memorial mentions Admiral Kimmel and General Short only once, and not at all disparagingly. Admiral Kimmel and General Short are not discussed prominently or disparagingly in history classes at West Point, Annapolis and the Air Force Academy. Of eight US history texts in use at the service academies today, one is critical of Admiral Kimmel. Thus, while their reputations may have been damaged in the years immediately following Pearl Harbor, the passage of time has produced balance.

5. There is not a compelling basis for advancing either officer to a higher grade.

a. Their superiors concluded that Admiral Kimmel and General Short did not demonstrate the judgment required of people who serve at the three- and four-star level. That conclusion may seem harsh, but it is made all the time. I have not seen a convincing basis for contradicting it in the instant case. It also is important to keep in mind that retirement at the two-star grade is not an insult or a stigma. Very few officers rise to that level of distinction.

b. Retirement at three- and four-star level was not a right in 1947 and is not today. Officers are nominated for retirement at that level by the President at the President's discretion and based on his conclusion that they served satisfactorily at the temporary grades. His nomination is subject to the advice and consent of the Senate. A nominee's errors and indiscretions must be reported to the Senate as adverse information.

I cannot conclude that Admiral Kimmel and General Short were victims of unfair official actions.

In sum, I cannot conclude that Admiral Kimmel and General Short were victims of unfair official actions and thus I cannot conclude that the official remedy of advancement on the retired list in order. Admiral Kimmel and General Short did not have all the resources they felt necessary.

Had they been provided more intelligence and clearer guidance, they might have understood their situation more clearly and behaved differently. Thus, responsibility for the magnitude of the Pearl Harbor disaster must be shared. But this is not a basis for contradicting the conclusion, drawn consistently over several investigations, that Admiral Kimmel and General Short committed errors of judgment. As commanders, they were accountable.

Admiral Kimmel and General Short suffered greatly for Pearl Harbor. They lost men for whom they were responsible. They felt that too much of the blame was placed on them. Their children and grandchildren continue to be haunted by it all. For all this, there can be sadness. But there can be no official remedy.

I recommend that you provide a copy of this memorandum and attachment to Senator Thurmond, the families of Admiral Kimmel and General Short, the secretaries of Army and Navy and other interested parties.

Edwin Dorn

Chapter 3

The Pearl Harbor Debate

1

In Defense of
Admiral Kimmel
and General Short

Vincent J. Colan

Loyalty is a highly prized virtue in the U.S. military. And there was little doubt about the loyalty, or the competence and dedication, of Admiral Husband E. Kimmel—at least until the Japanese attack on Pearl Harbor. Kimmel, the commander of the Pacific Fleet at the time of the attack, was demoted and eventually resigned from the service. He spent the rest of his life defending himself against charges arising from the Pearl Harbor disaster.

In the following article written for *Military* magazine, Captain Vincent J. Colan defends Kimmel's actions, and inaction, in late 1941. Colan finds that Kimmel was deprived of important information as well as the ships and planes he needed to defend the base. Colan also believes that Kimmel made a convenient scapegoat for the politicians in Washington, whose interest lay in covering up the facts surrounding Pearl Harbor and blaming the attack on the incompetence or inattention of commanders in the field.

To provide a brief perspective to my remarks, I would like to mention that I joined the Naval Reserve on my 18th birthday, 13 June 1932. In October '35, I joined the regular navy. After completing communication school at Norfolk Naval Base, VA, I reported aboard the USS *San Francisco* (CA38) in August '36, and was assigned to the signal bridge as a signalman.

From Vincent J. Colan, "Admiral Kimmel: The Pearl Harbor Scapegoat," *Military Magazine*, November 1998, December 1998, and January 1999. Reprinted with permission.

Bear in mind that unlike today's navy, warships before WWII did not have radar and sonar, or guided missiles controlled in combat centers located deep in the bowels of a ship. In the days before Pearl Harbor, admirals controlled their forces from the signal bridge of the flagship they were on. With ships' radios silent to avoid detection, battle orders and formation maneuvers were transmitted to other ships by visual communications from the signal bridge.

The USS *San Francisco* served as the flagship of Cruiser Division 7, consisting of the heavy cruisers *San Francisco*, *Tuscaloosa* and *Quincy*. From mid-1938 to mid-1939, Rear Admiral Kimmel was aboard as division commander. During this one-year period, I was in close proximity with the admiral, for literally he became a part of the signal gang.

During the frequent war games and formation exercises, he was always in the thick of the frantic activity that occurred on the signal bridge at these times. Rapid fire battle and formation signals were sent and received by flag hoists going up and down the yardarms, as well as by searchlight using Morse code, and by semaphore. Adm. Kimmel never waited the extra minutes for these signals and messages to be delivered to him in the plotting cabin. He wanted to be right there as they came in so that he could quickly respond with the required action. This tenacious compulsion to obtain and act on information without delay was a trait that never diminished in his later commands.

After his tour as commander Cruiser Division 7, Adm. Kimmel took command of Cruisers, Battle Force, United States Fleet. Then in early 1941, President Franklin Roosevelt, in announcing his appointment as commander in chief, Pacific, U.S. Fleet, with promotion to four-star admiral, praised him as "one of the greatest naval strategists of our time."

Shortly after the Japanese attack on Pearl Harbor, Adm. Kimmel was relieved of his command and reverted back to his permanent rank of two-star rear admiral. When it appeared that he would not receive orders to other commands, he requested retirement. From that time to the present, he and his family have lived in historical purgatory.

Adm. Kimmel had three sons, all of whom served in the navy during WWII. Tom Kimmel commanded four submarines during the war, and later commanded a heavy cruiser before retiring as a navy captain in 1965. Ned Kimmel entered the navy as a reserve ensign, and was a lieutenant commander when the war ended. Manning Kimmel was commanding officer of the submarine USS *Robalo*. In July 1944, while patrolling the South China Sea east of the Philippines, the *Robalo* struck a mine and sank with the loss of all hands. Tom and Ned Kimmel, and their sons, have struggled for the past 50 years to clear the admiral's name and have him restored to the rank he held before Pearl Harbor, that of four-star admiral.

Lt. Gen. Walter Short was the army commander in Hawaii at the time of the Pearl Harbor attack. His wife and son are dead. A grandson, Walter Short, is also attempting to have General Short's honor and rank restored. While the 1995 Senator [Strom] Thurmond hearing and the Pentagon Report, which will be discussed shortly, primarily emphasized the Kimmel case, the discussions, findings and conclusions in the above report dealt, to a smaller extent, with Gen. Short.

Intertwined in the events that led to Pearl Harbor are the terms "Naval Intelligence," "Purple Machine," and "Magic Messages." "Naval Intelligence" is the collection and dissemination of foreign naval operations and information into discriminating data that allows a decision-maker to act. A "Purple Machine" was the device used by allied cryptographers to decode the complex Japanese coded diplomatic messages. A "Magic Message" was the resultant decrypted message produced by the Purple Machine. In time, the decrypted messages were referred to as either Purple or Magic.

Only eight Purple machines were built. Army and Navy Intelligence in Washington had two each by August 1940. Winston Churchill received two in January 1941. One was sent to Admiral [Thomas] Hart and General [Douglas] MacArthur in the Philippines in April 1941. And then, in the summer of 1941 a third Purple was sent to Churchill. No Purple machine was ever sent to Adm. Kimmel in Pearl Harbor!

As a result of the release of vast quantities of WWII classified documents beginning in the 1970s, numerous books and articles have been published on the significance of these documents relating to the events leading to the Japanese attack on Pearl Harbor. For the most part, these books clearly show that an injustice had been done to Adm. Kimmel and Gen. Short. As a result, the Kimmel family, friends, authors and fellow admirals renewed their appeal to the Navy and Defense Departments to again consider the restoration of Adm. Kimmel to his four-star rank. When these departments refused to do so, they directed their appeal in early 1995 to Senator Strom Thurmond, chairman of the Senate Armed Services Committee.

Pentagon Report

On 25 Apr 95, a meeting was held by Senator Thurmond to hear testimony on this appeal. In attendance were high-ranking officials of the Navy and Defense Departments, members of the Kimmel family, historians and a number of retired admirals. At the conclusion of the meeting, the Navy and Defense Departments promised to come up with a speedy, fair and complete judgment on the matter. Eight months later, on 15 Dec 95, Defense officials submitted their report, hereafter called the Pentagon Report. It was released to the public on 3 Jan 96.

At the Senator Thurmond hearing in April 1995, General Counsel of the Navy Steve Honigman stated the reasons why the Navy and Defense Departments were opposed to the posthumous promotion of Adm. Kimmel from the two-star rank he reverted to after Pearl Harbor, to the four-star rank he held before. These reasons were overwhelmingly demolished by the facts presented by the Kimmel supporters present at the meeting. So much so, that the Pentagon officials involved in the examination of the Kimmel record jettisoned the weak first and third reasons Navy Counsel Honigman postulated, and widened the scope of the second reason he gave, that of committing "errors of judgment."

Let's take a look at the two reasons discarded by the Defense Department, because they were the pegs the Navy Department hung its scrambled eggs hat on for the past 50 years.

First reason—"The historical record does not establish convincingly that President Roosevelt, Gen. Marshall, or others in Washington deliberately withheld information from Adm. Kimmel and Gen. Short as part of a conspiracy to thrust America into the war."

This contention was never made by Adm. Kimmel or his family. It may have been made by historians, authors or others. If there is a "conspiracy" in the Adm. Kimmel case, it is the conspiracy being conducted by the Pentagon to withhold or suppress vital information that would clear Adm. Kimmel, and which would definitely point the finger at the culprits in Washington.

Third reason—Navy Counsel Honigman in the third reason postulated Three "Principles." We will take them up one at a time.

Principles

The first principle, he said, was the application of the naval service's principle of accountability of the commander, which made it proper to relieve Adm. Kimmel of command at Pearl Harbor. What Counsel Honigman conveniently ignores is the principle on the other side of the coin, which is, if a superior (meaning Chief of Naval Operations Adm. [Harold] Stark) fails to provide a subordinate (Adm. Kimmel) with available information and the forces to carry out his responsibilities, then that superior, not the subordinate, is at fault. In his book, "And I Was There," Adm. Edwin Layton, who was the intelligence chief at Pearl Harbor for both Adm. Kimmel and Adm. Chester Nimitz, said it best when he wrote, "By sending . . . snippets of Magic out of context, the Navy Department (Adm. Harold Stark, Chief of Naval Operations [CNO]) violated one of the cardinal rules of Intelligence: A local commander can only react to information in the context of his immediate situation. Thus, Washington had the advantage of constructing Tokyo's signals in the broader framework."

The second principle Navy Counsel gave was "the principle of the finality of judgment of Congress, prior Presidents, Secretaries of the Navy and of Defense." Here, he overlooks or ignores the fact that history is constantly being reviewed and revised as new information surfaces. There are a number of recent examples where this "principle of finality" gave way to new facts and evidence, such as the USS *Iowa* explosion, the sinking of the USS *Indianapolis*, and the USS *Pueblo* incident.

Also supporting Adm. Kimmel are numerous veterans organizations whose members saw service in WWII. These include members of the Pearl Harbor Survivors Association who were targets of the attack, and who were more aware of Kimmel's performance of duty before and during the attack than all the members of the committee who wrote the Pentagon Report released 3 Jan 96.

Without elaboration, and given little prominence in the Pentagon Report, is the comment, "Resources were scarce. The Navy in Hawaii was short of planes and crew." No kidding? It is incredible that this observation is meant to absolve Washington of any blame for its failures to provide Pearl Harbor with adequate forces, and blame Kimmel for not receiving the forces he needed.

Beginning in the early 1930s, for the first time since the end of WWI, new warships in the form of cruisers and destroyers were being built and added to the Pacific Fleet. With the advent of war in Europe, by the summer of 1941, a large number of ships of the Pacific Fleet were sent to the Atlantic Fleet. Adm. Kimmel lost 25% of his forces to the Atlantic Fleet by that time—one carrier, three battleships, four cruisers, 17 destroyers and 16 auxiliaries. Compounding Kimmel's problems, the navy weakened his remaining ships by transferring trained men and officers to man the new ships going to the Atlantic Fleet. Kimmel never received any of the new B-17s being built. They were all sent to [General Arthur] MacArthur in the Philippines, to London and to the Soviet Union. The record is clear. Over and over again, Adm. Kimmel wrote to CNO Adm. Stark pleading for additional personnel, ships and aircraft to contend with the developing situation in the Pacific, but his pleas were ignored.

Resources were scarce. The Navy in Hawaii was short of planes and crew.

The record is also clear. Both the military [army] and naval commanders at Pearl Harbor continuously conducted exhaustive offensive and defensive exercises with the limited assets they had available. They frequently conferred with each other and their staffs to fully execute the warnings and alerts received from Washington, which was then advised of the actions taken. When the Pearl Harbor commanders were not corrected or further advised, they felt that the actions taken were considered adequate. However, while they conferred frequently, it should be kept in mind that each had their own duties and responsibilities. Neither had the authority to give the other orders, or tell him how to carry out his duties.

Navy preparations for a war with Japan began in the early 1930s. Each year, up to the year before Pearl Harbor, the U.S. Fleet conducted war games, which had as their objective the defense of the Hawaiian Islands against a Japanese attack. In addition, the fleet spent more than the remaining half of the time at sea engaged in simulated battle problems, fleet and force tactics, gunnery and every other exercise simulating battle conditions. What little time was left was used for well-deserved leave and liberty for the crew, and upkeep and maintenance for the ships.

The hindsight charge that Adm. Kimmel failed to institute 360° patrols, extending 800 miles from Oahu, is ridiculous when you consider the meager forces he had available to conduct it. Not only were new bombers and patrol planes, intended for Pearl Harbor, being sent to MacArthur, but Washington was continually depleting Kimmel of a significant portion of his meager forces, which were sent to both the Atlantic Fleet and to the Philippines. To conduct those patrols, Kimmel needed at least 280 operational aircraft. He had only 49 worn out antiques with skeleton plane crews. A number of those planes were inoperable for lack of spare parts. To the extent they were able to do so, patrols were conducted around the immediate vicinity of the Hawaiian Islands.

On the morning of 7 December, contrary to widely published innuendoes that most of the ship's crews were ashore in drunken revelry in the bars of Honolulu, three quarters of each ship's crew were aboard their ships. Within five minutes of the surprise attack, all antiaircraft weapons were manned and firing. In retrospect, Adm. Kimmel and Gen. Short did a superb job, despite the wholly inadequate forces and information Washington had provided them.

Most of the public . . . having been apprised only of the alleged faults of Kimmel and Short, has retained that concept of Pearl Harbor.

Immediately after the Pearl Harbor attack, and further inflamed by selective negative portions of the reports of the Knox Investigation and the Justice Roberts Commission that were released to the public, hostility and hatred against the Pearl Harbor commanders rose to a fever pitch. Scathing indictments based on the emotional hysteria at the time, such as traitors, willful neglect and dereliction of duty were hurled at the Pearl Harbor commanders. Every penalty, from death to imprisonment, was called for. For 55 years, despite volumes of exonerating evidence being uncovered, most of the public, either having lived at that time, or having been apprised only of the alleged faults of Kimmel and Short, has retained that concept of Pearl Harbor.

As a result of extensive research by a number of historians and authors, a vast amount of evidence has been revealed that Kimmel and Short have been unfairly treated. The previous scathing indictments have now been reduced to "errors of judgment," which is the present basis used by the Pentagon to deny Kimmel and Short the ranks they previously held.

"Errors of Judgment"

The basis of the "errors of judgment" charge against Adm. Kimmel revolves around the actions taken, or not taken, in response to alerts and warnings allegedly sent to him by Washington. These alerts and warnings were the result of information Washington extracted from Magic messages decoded by the Purple machine as early as August 1940. In Washington, Magic messages were copied by Navy Radio, decoded by Naval Communications cryptographers, which, after analysis, sent copies to Navy War Plans for dissemination to proper officials and forces. Navy War Plans was headed by Rear Adm. Richmond Kelly Turner, who, as we will see, had some rather eccentric ideas as to who should get copies.

During all of 1941, Adm. Kimmel repeatedly wrote to CNO Adm. Stark in Washington, to be kept informed of everything concerning his command.

Repeatedly, Stark assured Kimmel he was sending everything he knew, and would continue to do so. However, the only messages Kimmel received from him were long, rambling and gossipy, hand-written letters. Occasionally Stark included a snippet of information from a Magic message, without revealing its source. These letters not only served to confuse Kimmel, but also actually misled him as to what Stark was trying to say. Clearly, these mailed letters which took weeks for delivery were no substitute for official, priority designated, coded messages sent by Navy Radio.

Security Leak

In June 1941, because of a suspected leak of a Magic message, officials in Washington clamped down on the distribution of Magic. From then on, Adm. Stark refrained from sending Kimmel even the confusing and misleading snippets of intelligence information gleaned from Magic. The clampdown extended even to President Roosevelt.

As many as 43 currently known vital and crucial Magic messages were denied to Adm. Kimmel. These included:

1. The "bomb plot" message of 9 October—In this message, and others that followed, Tokyo directed its consulate in Honolulu, using a special grid, to pinpoint on a daily basis the location of ships anchored or moored at Pearl Harbor, and to report arrivals and departures. No one in Washington thought this was important enough to alert Kimmel, so it was not sent to him. But it was sent to Adm. [Thomas] Hart, 5,000 miles away in the Philippines, who had a Purple machine and knew about it. In defense of Washington's inaction, the Pentagon Report second-guesses that Kimmel would not have taken any action regarding it.

2. The "winds message" of 28 November—In a message decoded by the Purple machine, Tokyo advised its consulates around the world of a weather code to indicate the breaking of diplomatic relations with the United States, England or the Soviet Union. It would appear in one of the daily Tokyo plain language weather reports. The code applicable to the United States was "East Wind Rain."

U.S. Army and Navy, as well as some allied radio stations around the world, were alerted to this code. Adm. Kimmel was alerted to this message, not from Washington, but from the commander of the Asiatic Fleet. Without having access to current Magic intercepts, and having received this from the Asiatic Fleet commander, it did not have the significance to the Hawaiian commanders that it had in Washington: that war was imminent. An "East Wind Rain" was discovered in a weather report transmitted from Tokyo on 3 December. This was copied by a number of radio stations around the world, including Washington. Fourteen copies of the message were known to have been typed, distributed to the proper officials, and then placed in the communication files of that office. Perhaps because that message was never sent to Kimmel, all copies mysteriously disappeared to give the impression that no such message was ever sent. Furthermore, since all messages were given a consecutive file number, no explanation was ever given as to what happened to each of the 14 messages missing from those files. Historians agree that had it been sent to Adm. Kimmel, it would have radically changed his estimate of the situation. The Pentagon Report denies that a "Winds Execute" message was ever received, and if it was, again second-guesses that Kimmel would have ignored it.

Warning

3. A "war warning" that originated in Washington was sent to all commands in the Pacific on 27 November 1941. It warned that an attack would probably be made on the Philippines, Malaysia or Borneo. Bear in mind that these places are not next door to Pearl Harbor, but 5,000 miles away. The "war warning" contained no specific directives as to how the Hawaiian commanders were to respond to the warning. Furthermore, without all the relevant intelligence that Washington had and never sent to Hawaii, this message was misleading because it was directed to the command in the Philippines, not to the commanders in Hawaii. Nevertheless, Kimmel and Short convened their staffs, reviewed and updated their sabotage defense plans, and advised Washington of their actions. When no response was received, the Pearl Harbor commanders concluded that the actions called for by the war warning message were satisfactory.

The feeling that Pearl Harbor was not the target was further buttressed by the order Adm. Kimmel received the same day as the war warning. He was ordered to use his only two carriers, escorted by a battleship, cruisers and destroyers, to ferry half his planes to Midway and Wake Islands. These planes were to be used to cover the impending arrival of 48 brand-new B-17 bombers being sent to General MacArthur in the Philippines. It had to be abundantly clear to all that Washington, in ordering Kimmel to dispatch a large portion of his ships and marine fighter planes to the Far East, was sending the message that there was no imminent threat to the Hawaiian Islands. Else, why would Washington send Kimmel's ships and aircraft, as well as 48 new bombers to the Philippines when they would be needed in Hawaii?

4. On 3 December, Adm. Kimmel received a dispatch addressed to the commander [of the] Asiatic Fleet for action and, get this, to Pearl Harbor for information! It advised Adm. Hart that Tokyo was ordering its embassies and legations to destroy their codes and coding machines, including those that Washington had named their Purple machines. He turned to his intelligence officer and asked, "What is Purple?" He didn't know, but would find out.

He asked a fleet security officer who recently arrived from Washington. Sworn to secrecy in the position he occupied there, he gave as skimpy a reply as possible, revealing nothing about the capabilities of the machine. He said it was a Japanese electric coding machine. Adm. Kimmel concluded that these machines were in the hands of only the Japanese. Foreign embassies of all nations destroyed their codes and machines from time to time, so what was so significant about this situation? Had he known that Washington, London and the Philippines also had Purple, and had been decoding Japanese diplomatic messages since August 1940, Kimmel certainly would have given the destroy message the significance it deserved. Here also, the Pentagon Committee downplayed what Kimmel's reaction might have been if he had known.

5. One more crucial Magic message is the "14 part message" Tokyo sent to its ambassador in Washington. The first 13 parts were decoded in Washington on 6 December, the day before Pearl Harbor. In those portions, Japan announced that it was rejecting Washington's compromise for peace in the Pacific. Upon reading the decrypts in his study in the White House that evening, President Roosevelt turned to his aide Harry Hopkins and said, "This means war." With the courier still in attendance, in the ensuing five or more minutes, no mention was made of Pearl Harbor, only of Indo-China.

These 13 parts were also delivered that day to Secretary of State Cordell Hull, Secretary of the Navy Knox, Secretary of the Army Stimson, CNO Adm. Stark, Army Chief of Staff Marshall, and to other high-ranking generals and admirals. While all gathered in their offices with their staffs to discuss the implications of the message, all arriving at the same conclusion as the President, no one thought to alert the commands in the field. While officials in Washington, in hindsight, expected Pearl Harbor to have been at "battle stations" since the war warning of 27 November, where was the leadership the night before the attack? President Roosevelt glanced at his stamp collection and then went to bed. General Marshall attended a reunion of WWI buddies. Adm. Stark went to the National Theatre to hear "The Student Prince."

The 14th part, called the "execute" part of the long message, was copied by Navy Radio at Washington early Sunday morning, 7 December. It was actually decoded hours before the Japanese embassy in Washington had done so. This part instructed the Japanese ambassador to deliver the position of the Japanese government, as set forth in the first 13 parts, to Secretary Hull at 1 p.m. that day, Sunday. Also, to report that it was breaking off relations with the United States. This way, Japan could claim that it did not violate the Geneva Convention by going to war with a country with which it had diplomatic relations. Bear in mind, that 1 p.m. in Washington was 8 a.m. in Honolulu.

Many dedicated army, navy and civilian officials had remained at their posts the night of 6 December; others returned early Sunday morning. The significance of the 1 p.m. time in the message became apparent to several army and navy officials. Recalling the Japanese custom of previous surprise attacks on a Saturday, Sunday, or holiday morning, and by looking at a time zone chart, 1 p.m. singled out Hawaii as the target of the attack. While most military and naval leaders were at their desks early Sunday morning, where was General Marshall, army chief of staff? He was horseback riding and couldn't be reached. An urgent message was left with his orderly to call his office at once. No one, army or navy dared to do anything without the personal approval of General Marshall.

About 10:30 that morning, a little more than two hours before the expected attack, Adm. [Theodore] Wilkinson, chief of naval intelligence, urged Adm. Stark to call and warn Kimmel. "No," he said, "I will call the President." The White House operator said he was not available. Stark put the phone in its cradle and did nothing more.

Also around 10:30, General Marshall finally called his office. He refused to take any messages, saying, "I am coming down to my office. You can give them to me then." He arrived there about 11:30 a.m. He ignored the frantic urgings of his aides for the immediate release of a war warning to the Pacific commanders. Instead, and before first reading the explosive "time of delivery" 14th part, Marshall, with the speed of a glacier, read the first 13 parts of the long message. At long last, he reached for a scrap of paper, and in an almost illegible scrawl, wrote a dispatch to be sent to army commands in the Philippines, the U.S. West Coast, Panama and Hawaii. He read the message to Adm. Stark who asked that it tell the army commands to "notify their Navy opposites," and offered to send it by the more powerful navy radio transmitters. Marshall insisted that army radio be used.

Despite the fact that Tokyo's "delivery message" clearly pointed to an attack on Hawaii, Marshall directed that transmission priority be given to MacArthur in the Philippines! Static interfered with the army's radio link to Hawaii. Mindful of Marshall's disdain for any navy participation in transmitting the message, the army aide gave it to Western Union for transmission to Fort Shafter in Hawaii. Incredibly, the coded message had not been assigned a priority handling designation, and thus it was given no more priority than a routine happy birthday greeting to a Pearl Harbor serviceman.

Upon receipt at Honolulu, it was pigeon-holed with other routine traffic and later given to a motorcycle messenger for delivery to Fort Shafter. On the way, bombs began falling and the messenger took shelter for about two hours before finally reaching his destination. By the time the message was decoded, it was eight hours after the attack when Gen. Short received the message. After sending a copy to Adm. Kimmel, he threw the original in a wastebasket. After receiving his copy, Kimmel did the same. Aides later retrieved both copies. . . .

Still a Scapegoat

The Pentagon Report concerning the Kimmel case was completed on 15 December 1995 and released on 3 January 1996. On the upside, the report was considered a significant step forward in the long battle by the Kimmel family to establish beyond a reasonable doubt that Kimmel and Short were not responsible for the Pearl Harbor disaster. For the first time since WWII, the U.S. government publicly confirmed that crucial messages were not sent to the Hawaiian commanders.

The report further reveals the ineptitude, unwarranted assumptions, misestimates, lack of leadership, organization and follow-up at the higher levels of command in Washington. The report unequivocally concludes with, "Responsibility for the Pearl Harbor disaster should not fall solely on the shoulders of Adm. Kimmel and Gen. Short; it should be broadly shared."

On the down side, the report abstains from arriving at the clear conclusions that Kimmel's "errors of judgment" were the inevitable consequences of the monumental blunders committed in Washington. The report recommended that the status quo of ranks not be disturbed—that neither Kimmel nor Short be posthumously promoted to their former ranks, and that nothing be done to disturb the higher ranks achieved by those in Washington as a result of their service after Pearl Harbor. In other words, the Pearl Harbor dishonor attached to the names of Kimmel and Short would remain, while not a blemish would be attached to the names of the Washington command. That can hardly be construed as "sharing the blame."

On 21 July 1997, Vice Adm. David C. Richardson, U.S. Navy Retired, issued a document, "A Critical Analysis Of The (Dorn) Report By The Department Of Defense . . ." which thoroughly and overwhelmingly rebutted every argument contained in the Dorn Report for denying Kimmel and Short their pre-WWII ranks. Vice Adm. Richardson is an experienced naval officer with a distinguished background serving in high fleet commands of the U.S. Navy.

Conclusion

The Kimmel family feels that after more than 50 years of struggle to clear the admiral's name and return him to his four-star rank, some progress has been made. It is apparent that under the current Clinton administration, nothing further can likely be achieved. The family, children, grandchildren and future generations will pursue the quest for complete vindication until it is obtained. To quote from a statement released by the Kimmel family, "If the Washington high command is entitled to wear four stars in the light of its performance, it seems clear that Adm. Kimmel is even more entitled to wear his four stars in the light of his performance than they are theirs."

If the Department of Defense refuses to right the grievous wrongs done to Adm. Kimmel and Gen. Short, and their families, then it is incumbent on the United States Senate to do so. Not only is the honor of the navy and the army at stake, but so is the honor of the United States.

2

An Indictment of Kimmel and Short

Henry C. Clausen and Bruce Lee

The investigation of Pearl Harbor in 1944 by the Army Pearl Harbor Board and the Naval Court of Inquiry did not satisfy those demanding a complete explanation of the Pearl Harbor attack. From certain information he received, Secretary of War Henry Stimson learned that military officers had probably lied on the witness stand for the sake of keeping military secrets and in particular to avoid revealing to Japan that the United States had broken its top-secret diplomatic message codes.

His confidence in the official findings shaken, Stimson asked San Francisco attorney Henry C. Clausen to undertake a private investigation of Pearl Harbor. With clearance to interview whomever he wished, and access to all decoded Japanese messages received in the months and weeks leading up to Pearl Harbor, Clausen was better informed than anyone else on the true events leading up to the attack. Clausen and his co-author, military historian Bruce Lee, offer their conclusions in the following passage from their book *Pearl Harbor: Final Judgment*.

The time had come for me to take the testimony of the Chief of Staff, George C. Marshall. . . .

I reviewed with Marshall the intercepts [of Japanese diplomatic messages] I carried with me. He said he believed before Pearl Harbor that [Gen. Walter] Short was aware of some of this information, and that Short was also receiving some other information from facilities available only in Hawaii. (By this, Marshall meant the messages from British intelligence that I had picked up in Hawaii.) As for Short's earlier testimony that the most important information he could have received would have been the news that the Japanese were destroying their codes, Marshall referred me to [Col. George W.] Bicknell's testimony. Bicknell had told me that the Navy had shown him on December 3 a cable from the Navy Department in Washington which read:

> Highly reliable information has been received that categoric and urgent instructions were sent yesterday to the Japanese diplomatic and consular posts at Hong Kong, Singapore, Batavia, Manila, Washington and London to destroy most of their codes and ciphers at once and to burn all other important confidential and secret documents.

Marshall reflected on this message and said: "It was customary and expected that information of this character would be exchanged between the respective services at Hawaii."

This puts the icing on the cake, I thought. I have taken the testimony of Captain [Edwin] Layton, the Pacific Fleet Intelligence Officer, who swore that it was against regulations to exchange this type of intelligence with the Army. Yet, here I have just heard the five-star general who has served for six years as Chief of Staff of the U.S. Army say that it "was customary and expected that information of this character would be exchanged between the respective services at Hawaii."

It attributes the lie or violation or disobedience to Layton—and to [Adm. Husband] Kimmel—in the most sweeping terms imaginable.

I must digress here for the moment. I don't believe any historian or any politician ever picked up on this point of who was telling the truth about these vital matters: Layton and Kimmel or Marshall. The reason for not doing so is obvious. In a single sentence, Marshall destroyed Layton's and Kimmel's arguments by showing how Layton and Kimmel had failed to do their duty. If you had Layton and Marshall testifying on this matter in a trial, the jury would side with Marshall, as it should. But the historians and politicians continue to ignore this, because it does not fit into their preconceived notions of conspiracy theories, or their ill-conceived plans for political revenge.

But to get back to Marshall's testimony: The Chief of

Staff would not elaborate on his statement to me. Nor would he make further comment on the fact that the Navy at Pearl Harbor had kept the second message of December 3, as well as the first one, from going directly to Short. Marshall was not going to engage in hindsight or speculation. He would deal only with fact. Marshall had already pointed out that Kimmel and Layton had failed to do their duty, and he rightly pointed out that Bicknell had also failed, even though he had had to rely on back-channel information that violated Top Secret regulations. Bicknell waited three days to present his news at a regular staff conference and then had watered down his report.

The real problem, which Marshall advanced with deadly clarity, was this: There were no relevant intelligence communications between Layton and Fielder, or between Kimmel and Short. The Pacific Fleet at Pearl Harbor had wanted to have everything its own way. It wanted to control intelligence information, and it did not share the information with Short's command, yet it wanted the Army to protect the fleet at Pearl Harbor. From my point of view, any further defense Layton or Kimmel might propose of their actions would be ludicrous.

Warnings to General Short

As for the types of warnings Marshall had personally given Short about the defense of his command, Marshall referred me to two letters he had sent Short. The first was dated February 7, 1941, and it said:

> My impression of the Hawaiian problem has been that if no serious harm is done us during the first six hours of known hostilities, thereafter the existing defenses would discourage an enemy against the hazard of an attack. The risk of sabotage, and the risk involved in a surprise raid by air and by submarine, constitute the real perils of the situation. Frankly, I do not see any landing threat in the Hawaiian Islands so long as we have air superiority.

A second letter from Marshall to Short, dated March 5, 1941, said:

> I would appreciate your early review of the situation in the Hawaiian Department with regard to defense from

air attack. The establishment of a satisfactory system of coordinating all means available to this end is a matter of first priority.

Marshall went on to point out that "estimates to the same general effect were sent to General Short by the War Department." The replies and other communications that the War Department received from Short indicated "that he was then alive to the danger of the possible surprise air attack against Pearl Harbor."

Marshall said all this with calm precision. His voice did not rise. Nor did anger show on his face. He delivered the coup de grace to Short by saying: "He participated in plans and exercises against such a possibility [of surprise air attack]. At no time did General Short inform me, or, to my knowledge, anyone else in the War Department that he was not in full agreement with these War Department estimates and plans for the defense of Oahu, which, in effect, warned him to expect air and submarine attacks as primary threats in the event of war with Japan."

What about Short's changing of the SOPs without having notified Washington?* I asked.

Said Marshall: "The doctrine of military command required that the Commanding General of an overseas command, such as the Hawaiian Department, must not act contrary to War Department estimates of the character mentioned, unless he believed such action to be dictated by necessity, and unless he immediately reported and gave full details and reasons to the War Department."

Since Short had changed the SOPs and reversed their order of importance without informing Washington, any confusion created by this, Marshall was saying, was Short's personal responsibility. Short's command's trying to hide the fact that these changes had been made without notifying Washington only made the situation worse.

I also believe that the two personal letters of instruction that Marshall had sent Short were ample directives to any general fearful of what to do, or unsure of what he was supposed to do. They were definitive in the respect that they predicted the exact thing that occurred, namely, a surprise air attack. Short should have been prepared to defend

---

* Ed. Note: Earlier, Clausen asserts that General Short changed the priority and numbering of alert statuses used by the Army's Hawaiian Department.

against an air attack by using long-range reconnaissance, whether by plane or by radar.

As it turned out, the Army's radar was not fully operational on December 7 when the attack occurred. Nor had an integrated air defense command system been established. Neither did Short make any effort to learn from Kimmel about the Navy's plans, or lack of plans, for long-range reconnaissance.

The debacle at Pearl Harbor was the result of Short's and Kimmel's being asleep at the switch.

Dereliction of Duty

Think of what would have happened if Short and Kimmel had been ready to fight.

When the Japanese attacked, they would have been met by our fighters in the air and antiaircraft guns blazing away from below. The Japanese might have sunk some of our ships, but our defenders would have been like the men at the Alamo, ready for an attack. If they were overwhelmed and killed, they would have been heroes. If they had kept the casualties down and saved some of the battleships from sinking, they would have been even greater heroes.

The fact of the matter was that our commanders and their forces were caught with their pants down. In war, you can't have it both ways. You can be a hero if you're ready to repel a surprise attack. You can't be a hero if you fail in your primary mission and suffer the casualties in personnel and the loss of matériel that we did.

The debacle at Pearl Harbor was the result of Short's and Kimmel's being asleep at the switch.

From what I had learned during my investigation, Short and Kimmel deserved to be relieved of their commands. Did they deserve harsher punishment? I believed so. *According to law, they appeared to be guilty of criminal negligence and dereliction of duty.*

Since this has been such a controversial matter for the past fifty years, let me pause a moment to explain. Let us use an auto accident as an example. Say you have a car that is defective. You put a bad driver in that car, and there is an accident. Had the driver been attentive, he might have avoided the accident. But, according to law, the driver should have known he had to be careful and look out for potentially dangerous situations; therefore, the accident occurred because the driver was violating his duty, and he is liable under the law. Now, the system that Kimmel and Short were operating under may have been faulty—indeed, I believe the system of handling Magic was improper—but both men were *ex industria* [purposefully] warned to be careful and avoid an accident, such as a surprise aerial attack. Neither man avoided the calamity. And neither man tried to communicate with the other about the potential dangers they jointly faced.

Let's put it another way: Kimmel and Short were like two sentries on duty who either did not look, and hence did not see, the tank that overran them, or who looked and still failed to see it. In either event, they were guilty of having failed to warn their comrades, and hence of dereliction of duty, just as a sentry on duty in time of war would be guilty and subjected to court-martial with the possibility of capital punishment.

Whether the military could accept this judgement remained to be seen. I was certain, however, that other civilian lawyers, such as Secretary [Henry] Stimson and Harvey Bundy, would agree with me. Indeed, they did.

If there was one mitigating factor in favor of Kimmel and Short, it was that, while they might have been sentries, it wasn't during a time of war that they failed in their duties, but in a time of peace. One might call it the result of the Pearl Harbor syndrome. Stephen Coonts is one of the first ex-military writers to touch on this, which he does in his best-selling novel *Under Siege*. Coonts's hero, Jake Grafton, explains why governments are caught with their pants down. "They weren't unprepared," Grafton says. "They just weren't ready, if you understand the difference. It's almost impossible for people who have known only peace to lift themselves to that level of mental readiness necessary to immediately and effectively counter a determined attack. . . . We refuse to believe."

3

The Roosevelt Administration Deliberately Provoked a Japanese Attack

Robert B. Stinnett

The questions and investigations on the subject of Pearl Harbor continued even as the century in which the attack took place came to an end. In the late 1990s, the U.S. Senate cleared Admiral Kimmel and General Short of wrongdoing, and the Pentagon officially declared that blame for unpreparedness at Pearl Harbor should be "broadly shared." While the latest investigations continued, journalist Robert B. Stinnett used the Freedom of Information Act to access thousands of formerly classified diplomatic and military documents. He examined intercepted and decrypted Japanese messages to discover who was privy to what information in the months before Pearl Harbor took place.

Stinnett concludes that Pearl Harbor was the end result of a high-level policy to deliberately provoke Japan into an attack on the United States. The policy closely followed the recommendations of Lt. Comdr. Arthur McCollum, head of the Far East Desk of the Office of Naval Intelligence. In October 1940, McCollum laid out an eight-part program that he believed would gradually goad Japan's belligerent military leaders into an attack. In his book *Day of Deceit*, Stinnett shows how the Roosevelt administration closely followed McCollum's plan, even as the United States proclaimed neutrality in the conflict between the Allies and the Axis powers.

Reprinted and abridged with the permission of The Free Press, a division of Simon & Schuster, Inc., from *Day of Deceit: The Truth About FDR and Pearl Harbor*, by Robert B. Stinnett. Copyright © 2000 by Robert B. Stinnett.

94

As warfare raged in Europe and portions of Africa and Japan, Germany and Italy threatened countries in three continents, a memorandum circulated in Washington. Originating in the Office of Naval Intelligence and addressed to two of FDR's most trusted advisors, it suggested a shocking new American foreign policy. It called for provoking Japan into an overt act of war against the United States. It was written by Lieutenant Commander Arthur H. McCollum, head of the Far East desk of the Office of Naval Intelligence (ONI).

McCollum had a unique background for formulating American tactics and strategy against Japan. Born to Baptist missionary parents in Nagasaki in 1898, McCollum spent his youth in various Japanese cities. He understood the Japanese culture, and spoke the language before learning English. After the death of his father in Japan, the McCollum family returned to Alabama. At eighteen McCollum was appointed to the Naval Academy. After graduation, the twenty-two-year-old ensign was posted to the US embassy in Tokyo as a naval attaché and took a refresher course in Japanese there. McCollum was no stuffed shirt. He enjoyed parties and the favorite drink of Japan's naval community—Johnny Walker Black Label Scotch. He was never at a loss for words. After telling a long story, he'd pause with his favorite phrases, "In other words," then go into an even longer version.

In 1923, as the fads of the Roaring Twenties swept the world, members of the Japanese imperial household were anxious to learn the Charleston. McCollum knew the latest dance routines, so the embassy assigned him to instruct Crown Prince Hirohito, the future Emperor, in slapping his knees to those jazz-age rhythms. Later that year, McCollum helped coordinate the US Navy relief operations following the great Tokyo earthquake. Though the American assistance was well intentioned, McCollum learned that the proud, self-sufficient Japanese resented the *anjin* (foreign) relief operations. Nearly twenty years later, McCollum took it upon himself to multiply this resentment a hundredfold by pushing for American interference in Japan's brutal policies of domination in the Pacific.

The Eight-Action Memo

Lieutenant Commander McCollum's five-page memorandum of October 1940 (hereafter referred to as the eight-action memo) put forward a startling plan—a plan intended to engineer a situation that would mobilize a reluctant America into joining Britain's struggle against the German armed forces then overrunning Europe. Its eight actions called for virtually inciting a Japanese attack on American ground, air, and naval forces in Hawaii, as well as on British and Dutch colonial outposts in the Pacific region.

Opinion polls in the summer of 1940 indicated that a majority of Americans did not want the country involved in Europe's wars.

Opinion polls in the summer of 1940 indicated that a majority of Americans did not want the country involved in Europe's wars. Yet FDR's military and State Department leaders agreed that a victorious Nazi Germany would threaten the national security of the United States. They felt that Americans needed a call to action.

McCollum would be an essential part of this plan. His code name was F-2. He oversaw the routing of communications intelligence to FDR from early 1940 to December 7, 1941, and provided the President with intelligence reports on Japanese military and diplomatic strategy. Every intercepted and decoded Japanese military and diplomatic report destined for the White House went through the Far East Asia section of ONI, which he oversaw. The section served as a clearinghouse for all categories of intelligence reports, not only on Japan but on all the other nations of eastern Asia.

Each report prepared by McCollum for the President was based on radio intercepts gathered and decoded by a worldwide network of American military cryptographers and radio intercept operators. McCollum's office was an element of Station US, a secret American cryptographic center located at the main naval headquarters at 18th Street and Constitution Avenue N.W., about four blocks from the White House.

Few people in America's government or military knew as much about Japan's activities and intentions as Lieutenant Commander Arthur H. McCollum. He felt that war with Japan was inevitable and that the United States should provoke it at a time which suited US interests. In his October 1940 memorandum McCollum advocated eight actions that he predicted would lead to a Japanese attack on the United States:

A. Make an arrangement with Britain for the use of British bases in the Pacific, particularly Singapore.

B. Make an arrangement with Holland for the use of base facilities and acquisition of supplies in the Dutch East Indies [now Indonesia].

C. Give all possible aid to the Chinese government of Chiang Kai-shek.

D. Send a division of long-range heavy cruisers to the Orient, Philippines, or Singapore.

E. Send two divisions of submarines to the Orient.

F. Keep the main strength of the US Fleet, now in the Pacific, in the vicinity of the Hawaiian Islands.

G. Insist that the Dutch refuse to grant Japanese demands for undue economic concessions, particularly oil.

H. Completely embargo all trade with Japan, in collaboration with a similar embargo imposed by the British Empire .

McCollum's eight-action memo was dated October 7, 1940, and was addressed and forwarded to two of Roosevelt's most trusted military advisors: Navy captains Walter S. Anderson and Dudley W. Knox. Anderson was the Director of the Office of Naval Intelligence and had direct White House access to FDR. Knox was a naval strategist and chief of the ONI library. He served as mentor to Admiral Ernest J. King, another of the President's military advisors in 1940–41 and commander of the Navy's Atlantic Squadron (later the Atlantic Fleet). Knox agreed with McCollum's eight actions and immediately forwarded the memorandum to Anderson with this restrained comment: "I concur in your courses of action. We must be ready on both sides and probably strong enough to care for both." He recognized Britain's precarious military position: "It is unquestionably to our general interest that Britain be not licked. Just now she has a stalemate and probably can't do better." Knox did not discuss maneuvering Japan into committing an overt act of war, though he cautioned: "We should not precipitate anything in the Orient."

The paper trail of the McCollum memo ends with the Knox endorsement. Although the proposal was addressed to Anderson, no specific record has been found by the author indicating whether he or Roosevelt actually ever saw it." However, a series of secret presidential routing logs plus collateral intelligence information in Navy files offer conclusive evidence that they did see it. Beginning the very next day, with FDR's involvement, McCollum's proposals were systematically put into effect.

Fingerprints

Throughout 1941, it seems, provoking Japan into an overt act of war was the principal policy that guided FDR's actions toward Japan. Army and Navy directives containing the "overt act" phrase were sent to Pacific commanders. Roosevelt's cabinet members, most notably Secretary of War Henry Stimson, are on record favoring the policy, according to Stimson's diary. Stimson's diary entries of 1941 place him with nine other Americans who knew or were associated with this policy of provocation during 1941.

Roosevelt's "fingerprints" can be found on each of McCollum's proposals. One of the most shocking was Action D, the deliberate deployment of American warships within or adjacent to the territorial waters of Japan. During secret White House meetings, Roosevelt personally took charge of Action D. He called the provocations "pop-up" cruises: "I just want them to keep popping up here and there and keep the Japs guessing. I don't mind losing one or two cruisers, but do not take a chance on losing five or six." Admiral Husband Kimmel, the Pacific Fleet commander, objected to the pop-up cruises, saying: "It is ill-advised and will result in war if we make this move."

One of the catalysts for Action D may have been British Prime Minister Winston Churchill. On October 4, 1940, he requested that a squadron of U.S. cruisers be sent to Singapore. McCollum included the request as a suggestion in his eight-action memo. As it turned out, however, no cruisers were sent to Singapore.

From March through July 1941, White House records show that FDR ignored international law and dispatched naval task groups into Japanese waters on three such "pop-up cruises." One of the most provocative was a sortie into the Bungo Strait southeast of Honshu, the principal access to Japan's Inland Sea. The strait separates the home islands of Kyushu and Shikoku, and was a favored operational area for the warships of the Imperial Japanese Navy in 1941.

Japan's naval ministry registered a protest with Ambassador Joseph Grew in Tokyo: "On the night of July 31, 1941, Japanese fleet units at anchor in Sukumo Bay (in the Bungo Strait, off the island of Shikoku) picked up the sound of propellers approaching Bungo Channel from the eastward. Duty destroyers of the Japanese navy investigated and sighted two darkened cruisers that disappeared in a southerly direction behind a smoke screen when they were challenged." The protest concluded: "Japanese naval officers believe the vessels were United States cruisers."

Action D was very risky and could have resulted in a loss of American lives approaching that of Pearl Harbor. In the end, however, no shots were fired during the cruises. It would take not just one, but all eight of McCollum's proposals to accomplish that.

Action F

Two major decisions involving Japan and the Far East took place on October 8, 1940—the day after McCollum wrote his memo. First, the State Department told Americans to evacuate Far East countries as quickly as possible. Then President Roosevelt brought about Action F—keep the United States Fleet based in Hawaiian waters—during an extended Oval Office luncheon with the fleet's commander, Admiral James O. Richardson, and former Chief of Naval Operations Admiral William D. Leahy, a favored presidential confidant. When Richardson heard the proposal, he exploded: "Mr. President, senior officers of the Navy do not have the trust and confidence in the civilian leadership of this country that is essential for the successful prosecution of a war in the Pacific." Richardson did not approve of Roosevelt's plan to place the fleet in harm's way. He strongly disagreed with two of FDR's lunchtime points: 1. FDR's willingness to sacrifice a ship of the Navy in order to provoke what he called a Japanese "mistake," and 2. Richardson quoted the President as saying: "Sooner or later the Japanese would commit an overt act against the United States and the nation would be willing to enter the war."

After Richardson and Leahy left the Oval Office luncheon, dishes were cleared and reporters were ushered in for a 4:00 P.M. press conference. The ever-affable FDR used humor to lead reporters astray:

Q: Can you tell us anything, Mr. President, about your conference this afternoon with Admiral Richardson and Admiral Leahy?

THE PRESIDENT: Oh, we were just studying maps.

Q: Did the conference touch upon frontiers in the Far East?

THE PRESIDENT: We studied maps.

Q: Pacific maps?

THE PRESIDENT: We studied maps and are learning geography.

Q: Were they mostly in the Eastern Hemisphere?

THE PRESIDENT: What?

Q: We thought mostly maps of the Eastern Hemisphere.

THE PRESIDENT: All three hemispheres.

Q: O.K. (*Laughter*)

For Richardson, the safety of his men and warships was paramount and the policy was no laughing matter. Richardson stood up to Roosevelt. Doing so ended his naval career. On October 26, 1940, a White House leak to the Washington-based *Kiplinger Newsletter* predicted that Richardson would be removed as commander-in-chief.

The admiral was relieved of his command on February 1, 1941, during a major restructuring of the Navy. The sea command held by Richardson—Commander in Chief, United States Fleet (CINCUS)—was modified. In his restructuring, Roosevelt approved a two-ocean Navy and created the Atlantic Fleet and the Pacific Fleet. Skipping over more senior naval officers the President picked Rear Admiral Husband Kimmel to head the Pacific Fleet and promoted him to four-star rank. The job had been offered to Rear Admiral Chester Nimitz in the fall of 1940, but Nimitz "begged off" because he lacked seniority.

An All Too Faithful Servant

Roosevelt had carefully selected and placed naval officers in key fleet command positions who would not obstruct his provocation policies. One of them was Admiral Harold Stark, his chief of naval operations since August 1939, an all too faithful servant of the President. Outgoing Admiral Richardson criticized Stark as "professionally negligent" for kowtowing to FDR and agreeing to place the fleet in jeopardy. He said Stark had been derelict and had suffered a major professional lapse due to "taking orders from above." In Richardson's opinion, Stark could have protested the orders to keep the fleet at Pearl Harbor or at least questioned the policy in proper but forceful fashion. After the success of the December 7 attack, Richardson claimed FDR turned his back on Stark: "The President said that he did not give a damn what happened to Stark so long as he was gotten out of Washington as soon as practical."

There is no evidence that Admiral Kimmel knew of the action plans advocated by McCollum, because Admiral Richardson never told him of them. "The Roosevelt strategy of maneuvering the Japanese into striking the first blow at America was unknown to us," Kimmel wrote in his book, *Admiral Kimmel's Story*, published in 1954. His first suspicions that someone in high office in Washington had consciously pursued a policy that led straight to Pearl Harbor "did not occur to him until after December 7, 1941." Kimmel said he accepted the command of the Pacific Fleet "in the firm belief that the Navy Department would supply me promptly with all pertinent information available and particularly with all information that indicated an attack on the fleet at Pearl Harbor."

Not until Japan surrendered in 1945 did Richardson break his four-year vow of silence and turn on Stark. He said he shared Kimmel's belief and he denounced Stark's failure in harsh terms: "I consider 'Betty' Stark, in failing to ensure that Kimmel was furnished all the information available from the breaking of Japanese dispatches, to have been to a marked degree professionally negligent in carrying out his duties as Chief of Naval Operations." Richardson continued: "This offense compounded, since in writing Stark had assured the Commander-in-Chief of the United States Fleet twice that the Commander-in-Chief was being kept advised on all matters within his own knowledge." Richardson cited Stark's promise:

"You may rest assured that just as soon as I get anything of definite interest, I shall fire it along."

Kimmel received his promotion to admiral and was designated CINCPAC (Commander in Chief, Pacific Fleet).

Then, depending upon their missions, forces were either assigned to the Atlantic Fleet, whose commander was Admiral Ernest J. King as CINCLANT, to the Pacific Fleet with Kimmel as CINCPAC, or to the small Asiatic Fleet, commanded by Admiral Thomas Hart in Manila as CINCAF.

The Back-Door Approach

Richardson's removal on February 1, 1941, strengthened the position of McCollum. Only five months earlier, in mid-September 1940, Germany and her Axis partner, Italy, had signed a mutual-assistance alliance with Japan. The Tripartite Pact committed the three partners to assist each other in the event of an attack on any one of them. McCollum saw the alliance as a golden opportunity. If Japan could be provoked into committing an overt act of war against the United States, then the Pact's mutual assistance provisions would kick in. It was a back-door approach: Germany and Italy would come to Japan's aid and thus directly involve the United States in the European war.

McCollum predicted a domino effect if Germany overwhelmed Britain. He was certain that Canada and the British territories in Central and South America and in the Caribbean would succumb to some degree of Nazi control. The strategic danger to the United States was from Germany, not Japan. In his eight-action memorandum, McCollum cited these six military factors in promoting his proposals:

1. All of continental Europe was under the military control of the German-Italian Axis.
2. Only the British Empire actively opposed the growing world dominance of the Axis powers.
3. Axis propaganda successfully promoted American indifference to the European war.
4. United States security in the Western Hemisphere was threatened by the Axis fomenting revolution in Central and South American countries.
5. Upon the defeat of England, the United States could expect an immediate attack from Germany.
6. Warships of the Royal Navy would fall under the control of the Axis when the British were defeated.

His dire predictions were undoubtedly right. The number one problem for the United States, according to McCollum, was mobilizing public support for a declaration of war against the Axis powers. He saw little chance that Congress would send American troops to Europe. Over the objection of the majority of the populace, who still felt that European alarmists were creating much ado about nothing, he called for the Administration to create what he called "more ado": "It is not believed," wrote McCollum, "that in the present state of political opinion the United States government is capable of declaring war against Japan without more ado."

His solution to the political stalemate: use the eight proposed actions to provoke Japan into committing an overt act of war against the United States, thus triggering military responses from the two other signers of the Tripartite Pact.

4

Roosevelt Did Not Deliberately Provoke a Japanese Attack

Donald M. Goldstein and Katherine V. Dillon

Of all the Pearl Harbor scholars, Professor Gordon W. Prange of the University of Maryland, and former chief of the historical section in Japan under General MacArthur, may have worked the hardest. Prange put in 37 years of research in the United States and Japan and personally interviewed every major surviving figure of the Pearl Harbor story. His life's work resulted in *At Dawn We Slept*, an incredibly detailed and comprehensive book that remains the standard reference work on Pearl Harbor for students, scholars, and the general public.

Unfortunately, Prange's death in 1980 prevented him from fully addressing the conspiracy theories and revisionist accounts that faulted President Roosevelt for knowing about, or deliberately provoking, the Pearl Harbor attack. But in an appendix to *At Dawn We Slept*, his collaborators Katherine V. Dillon and Donald M. Goldstein summarize chapters of the original manuscript that did not appear in the final version. The summary deftly analyzes, and handily defeats, the assumptions, leaps of faith, faulty logic, and conspiratorial mindset that led the Pearl Harbor revisionists to their dubious conclusions.

<hr />

In Chapters 139 through 143 of his original manuscript for Volume Four of his book, Gordon Prange discussed the revisionist school at great length. The following is a summary:

While the Pearl Harbor attack united the American people, it was too much to ask that unity in the war effort would also create political unity. The legend began that Pearl Harbor was Roosevelt's fault—a legend that flourished in the postwar revisionist school.

The more reasonable revisionists confined themselves to criticism of Roosevelt's approach to foreign affairs. William L. Neumann [in his article "How American Policy Towards Japan Contributed to War in the Pacific"] believed that American foreign policy before World War II was unsound because the Soviet Union was the ultimate gainer." The major thrust of William Henry Chamberlin's book *America's Second Crusade* was that if the United States had kept out of the war, communism would have been contained.

Neumann's and Chamberlin's conclusions were arguable for two reasons. First, a President and his State Department cannot be lords of the future. And in 1941 any menace to the United States from the Russians and the Chinese was problematical, while the threat from the Nazis and the Japanese militarists was immediate. Secondly, their theses tacitly implied that if the United States stood aside while Hitler swallowed the British Empire and the Soviet Union, *der Führer* thereupon would settle down with a contented sigh, and the Third Reich and the United States would coexist like the lion and the lamb. Even the most cursory look at Hitler's record makes this notion questionable.

Pruning the Evidence

Another brand of revisionists believed that Roosevelt deliberately dragged the United States into the war. This group stopped short of claiming that he schemed to have the Japanese attack Pearl Harbor. For example, Charles A. Beard, in *President Roosevelt and the Coming of the War 1941*, wrote a blistering indictment of Roosevelt, his administration, and in particular, his foreign policy. According to Beard, the President was a warmonger who deceived the American people, violated his antiwar campaign pledge of 1940, and maneuvered the Japanese into firing the first shot.

Nowhere in his book did Beard directly accuse Roosevelt of knowing that the Japanese were going to attack Pearl Harbor. But he made his points in a subtle and sophisticated way. Without actually misquoting, he judiciously pruned the evidence. For example, he wrote, "Secretary Stimson testified before the Army Pearl Harbor Board that he was not surprised by the Japanese attack—on Pearl Harbor." Here is the actual exchange in question: [Army Board member Henry] Russell asked Stimson, "Then you were not surprised at the air attack on the 7th of December?" Stimson replied, "Well, I was not surprised, in one sense, in any attack that would be made; but I was watching with considerably more care, because I knew more about it, the attack that was framing up in the southwestern Pacific. . . ." This conveys quite a different impression from Beard's selective extract.

[In his article "The Pearl Harbor Investigations"] Percy L. Greaves, Jr., too, conceded, "Washington did not know, or at least no evidence has been adduced that Washington knew, precisely, that the attack would fall on Pearl Harbor although they [sic] had good reason to expect that it might."

John T. Flynn, in his pamphlet *The Truth About Pearl Harbor*, believed that the President "wanted to provoke Japan to attack. But he . . . certainly never looked for an attack that would kill 3,000 Americans and knock the American Navy and Army out of the war in a day. . . ."

Harry Elmer Barnes was the leading spirit of the thesis that Roosevelt had planned the whole thing deliberately, knew about the attack on Pearl Harbor in advance, and wanted it to happen. He believed the President guilty of a triple conspiracy. First, Roosevelt needed an attack on this country because of his campaign promise that Americans would not be sent to war unless the United States was attacked. Secondly, to permit such an attack unobstructed, he arranged that Kimmel and Short should receive none of the information available in Washington from Japanese decoded material. Thirdly, he conspired to cover up the failure to warn the Hawaiian commanders.

A surprising number of naval personnel interviewed for this study fell into the Roosevelt-planned-it category. To such dedicated Navy men it seemed impossible that the U.S. Pacific Fleet could have been so appallingly surprised and defeated unless treachery had been involved, and they identified with Kimmel's interests. ". . . I am glad to learn you are going ahead on Kimmel," wrote Rear Admiral Dundas P. Tucker to Lieutenant Commander Charles C. Hiles on June 2, 1968, "because you will be clearing not only him, but the professional Navy as a whole. . . ."

Careless Facts

Some of the more vociferous revisionists were careless with facts. Although Chamberlin's book was published in 1950, by which time the composition of Nagumo's task force was known, Chamberlin stated that it was "under the command of Admiral Isoroku Yamamoto. . . ." Such a mistake* is not evidence of bad faith, but it is the sort of factual error that casts doubt upon a historian's credibility. Chamberlin also wrote, "As early as November 28 it was known in Washington that a Japanese flotilla . . . was steaming down the China coast toward an unknown destination. Only the main objective of the impending offensive, Pearl Harbor . . . did not visibly figure in Japanese calculations." Of course, this fleet was not the one headed for Hawaii, as a glance at the map would show. Further, Chamberlin would have us believe that "the commanders on the spot were encouraged to maintain a normal, 'business as usual' attitude until the attack actually took place. . . ." This was far from the case.

Some of the more vociferous revisionists were careless with facts.

Rear Admiral Robert A. Theobald's book *The Final Secret of Pearl Harbor* was the quintessence of revisionism. It pictured the Navy as a collective Andromeda chained to the rock of Pearl Harbor while Roosevelt and subsidiary vultures Stimson, Marshall, *et al.* hovered around, waiting for the Japanese dragon to play its predestined part. In reviewing this book, Commander Masataka Chihaya, formerly of the Imperial Japanese Navy, put his finger on the key weakness of this position: "Even if one admits Adm. Theobald's assertion that President Roosevelt wanted to have Japan strike first, there would have been no need to have all the major ships of the U.S. Fleet sit idly in the harbor to be mercilessly destroyed and many killed."

Such a blood sacrifice was by no means necessary to force the American people to accept entry into the war. The loss of men, ships, and planes grieved and shocked the na-

---

* Ed. Note: Nagumo, and not Yamamoto, was commander of the Pearl Harbor striking force.

tion; what angered it, as we have seen, was Japan's striking under cover of diplomacy before declaring war.

No such considerations disturbed Barnes. According to him, when Hitler did not oblige by attacking the United States:

> . . . it became essential for Roosevelt to do all possible to assure that Japan would provide the indispensable attack that was needed to unite the American people behind him in the war. To bring this about it appeared necessary to prevent Hawaiian commanders from taking any offensive action which would deter the Japanese from attacking Pearl Harbor which, of necessity had to be a surprise attack.

This peculiar concept ignores two facts: The Japanese never expected Operation Hawaii to be a shoo-in, and the reason for the Hawaiian Department's existence was to protect the Fleet and the Islands against a Japanese attack.

Therefore, if the President planned to enter the war by the so-called back door, every dictate of common sense urged that he take Kimmel and Short into his confidence, at least to the extent of warning them that the Japanese were coming. In that case, the Pacific Fleet's carrier task forces would have been lying in wait, reinforced by the battleships; the radar systems would have been operating at full strength; reconnaissance aircraft, destroyers, and submarines would have been scouting the area; antiaircraft batteries would have been in position with ammunition at the ready; the Hawaiian Air Force's planes would have been fueled, armed, and poised for immediate takeoff. Under those circumstances Pearl Harbor could have been an entirely different story, as the Japanese acknowledge.

"Just Go Home"

Barnes assumed that if Nagumo knew his target had been alerted, he would have called off the strike. Research shows that during [Rear Admiral Ryunosuke] Kusaka's briefing at Hitokappu Bay the admiral stated that if the enemy sighted the task force before X-Day minus one, Nagumo would return to Japan. But if the Americans spotted only part of the Japanese fleet, Nagumo would change course and proceed toward Oahu. Moreover—and this is most important—if fired on, the Japanese would fight it out. [Commander Minoru] Genda echoed these instructions. But it is difficult to regard as realistic the suggestion that Operation Hawaii would or could have been aborted had the Americans discovered the task force before December 6. Nothing in the planning and training for the venture lends credence to the idea that Nagumo was to scratch the mission if sighted.

If the President planned to enter the war by the so-called back door, every dictate of common sense urged that he take Kimmel and Short into his confidence.

Barnes's theory assumes that Nagumo had complete control of the situation and could go ahead or turn homeward at will. But on December 6 Nagumo was well east of Midway, heading southeast. That night he turned due south. Even in the best of times a Japanese carrier task force would have difficulty explaining its presence in that location. It is absurd to suggest that in December 1941 a U.S. fleet encountering Nagumo's armada would figuratively say, "Anybody can get lost. Just go home and no harm done."

Then, too, the whole object of the attack was to destroy Kimmel's ships wherever they might be found, in port or at sea. In fact, the Japanese would have preferred to sink their prey in waters deep enough to swallow them forever. Therefore, it is probable that had Nagumo encountered a U.S. task force while he was en route to Pearl Harbor, he would have attacked at once, not turned tail.

Most important, a ready foe was precisely what Nagumo expected. Yamamoto had instructed him and his officers that they must be prepared to fight their way in to the target. When they actually did achieve complete surprise, the Japanese were as amazed as they were elated.

In brief, Barnes and some of his followers indulged in a prime example of reverse logic. With all the force at their command, these people wanted to prove Roosevelt guilty of Pearl Harbor. To do so, they had to convince the public that the President deliberately withheld information from Kimmel and Short. And the only way to make sense of that concept was to hypothesize that the Japanese would have turned back if detected.

What Ifs

Yet had Kimmel taken the actions which the Navy Department expected when it issued the war warning of November 27, he would have been alerted and scouting his sea area for possible intruders. Suppose he found them? Stark, no firebrand, testified that if the enemy were spotted within 800 miles north of Oahu, he would have fired. No doubt the much more aggressive Kimmel would have done the same. Failure to do so would have, in [General Leonard] Gerow's words, "jeopardized his defense" and constituted failure to obey the warning contained in the message of November 27.

Neither Stark nor Gerow considered such a forceful meeting of an obvious peril to constitute an "overt act" within the meaning of the warning message. While Washington wanted the Japanese to bear the onus of aggression, it certainly did not intend Kimmel and Short to stand still to be attacked if they knew danger was approaching. Had the defenders of Hawaii discovered and tried to fight off the Japanese task force, there would have been the shooting war, without the element of surprise and with no help from Roosevelt.

If the revisionists claimed that the President lured the Japanese into sending the bulk of their carrier strength across the Pacific so that the U.S. Navy could destroy it, this would make sense strategically. It would be Japan's Great All-Out Battle concept in reverse. However, Prange thought it an absurdity to assert that Roosevelt risked the prime units of the U.S. Pacific Fleet—the very tactical tools the United States would need in a Pacific conflict—to justify a declaration of war.

Kimmel attempted to reconcile this incongruity with his own firm conviction of Roosevelt's and Marshall's guilt. In an interview with Neumann, Kimmel stated that he did not believe they "wanted to sacrifice the Pacific Fleet." He thought, as did Neumann, that ". . . they assumed that one American could deal with five Japanese and that even a surprise attack would be beaten off without great losses. . . ."

Nevertheless, if by some quirk of logic one could accept tethering a few obsolescent battleships in Pearl Harbor to tempt the Japanese, one boggles at the idea of staking out the whole military establishment on Oahu for that purpose. The revisionist position implied that Roosevelt and his advisers knew that the Japanese would hit the ships rather than the much more strategically and logistically important shore installations and fuel supply. Washington had no way to determine this. In fact, sound strategy dictated the reverse and, as we have seen, all concerned could not believe that the attackers would sail away without striking these vital targets.

Furthermore, any "baiting" on Roosevelt's part presumably would be aimed at Tokyo's foreign policy level, including the War and Navy ministries and indirectly the General Staffs. Yet those were the very elements that fought the Pearl Harbor plan tooth and nail. The President could not hypnotize Yamamoto into planning to attack Pearl Harbor and imbue him with the courage to buck the Naval General Staff.* Certainly Roosevelt could not foresee that organization's folding up under Yamamoto's threat to resign.

Another consideration reduced the extreme revisionist thesis to its ultimate absurdity. How could the President ensure a successful Japanese surprise attack unless he confided in the Hawaiian commanders and persuaded them to allow the enemy to proceed unhindered? Kimmel's and Short's business was to be on the alert at all times. Roosevelt would have to assume that the Hawaiian outpost would be on its toes. To carry the revisionist theory to its logical conclusion, one would have to include as parties to the plot Kimmel, Short, their subordinate commanders, and key members of their staffs. In no other way could the alleged plotters have ensured that the Japanese would come in unopposed.

Sheer Scurrility

One of the principal, if unofficial, objectives of the [1946] congressional committee [inquiry] was to clarify Roosevelt's role in relation to Pearl Harbor. But a number of publications had already made up their minds. In September 1945 John Chamberlain asserted in *Life*, ". . . Roosevelt . . . knew in advance that the Japanese were going to attack us. There is even ground for suspicion that he elected to bring the crisis to a head when it came."

For sheer scurrility, however, we could award the wreath of poison ivy to a small Chicago newspaper, *Women's Voice*, which editorialized on December 27, 1951, concerning al-

---

* Ed. Note: Japanese naval commanders originally resisted plans to attack Pearl Harbor.

leged events on Oahu: "The order the night before, to go into town, to get drunk. . . . Those who returned to the ships in the night were kept from coming on board by officers with drawn revolvers. . . ." Planes had been defueled "to make absolutely sure that no plane could be gotten into the air. . . ." A staff sergeant, prudently unidentified, claimed that he did take off in his aircraft. And what did he find? ". . . planes manned by white men, men whom I knew—British and Americans. There seemed to be a few Japs, but the shooting was done by white men. . . ." Three other young men contributed enthusiastically to this myth: "There were Jap planes mixed in, but a lot of them did not shoot, and we afterward found they were photo fellows. . . ."

A "civilian contractor" put on the capstone: "He said it was well known that Roosevelt with Churchill's help planned the whole thing, and called in the Japs to help, promising them the Philippine Islands." That remark really ties up the revisionist package with a neat bow. If one believes this article, Roosevelt did not merely bait the Japanese into attacking; he bribed them into partnership. And the Japanese did not truly attack at all; the Americans with a few British did it. The Japanese just trailed along to take pictures.

Another widely circulated myth claimed that Roosevelt knew about the Pearl Harbor attack well in advance thanks to the Soviet Union. This tale credits Richard Sorge, head of the famous communist spy ring in Tokyo, with learning about Japan's plan to strike Hawaii and passing the information to Moscow, which thereupon informed Washington. A host of correspondents and writers bought this yarn and from it wove a whole fabric of indictments and unverified conclusions. However, a slight tug at the end of the yarn unravels the whole fabric. Research reveals that Sorge did not crack the Pearl Harbor secret, hence could not advise Moscow, which hence could not advise Washington, which hence could not sit on the information.

The Roosevelt-as-villain thesis tacitly assumed that if Pearl Harbor had not occurred, the United States would not have entered the war. Yet if the [Japanese] Naval General Staff had vetoed Yamamoto's plan or if, once under way, Nagumo had aborted the air attack, the political situation between the two countries would not have changed. Precisely the same forces that launched the war would have remained—the same tensions between Tokyo and Washington, the same conflicts of interest, the same ideological antagonisms, the same determination on Japan's part to absorb Southeast Asia into its Co-Prosperity Sphere, the same American commitment to China; the same obligation on the part of Washington to protect American territory and citizens outside the continental United States.

Japan's massive Southern Operation for the conquest of Southeast Asia and command of the western Pacific was under way well before December 7, 1941. And that offensive included an attack on U.S. forces in the Philippines preparatory to taking over the islands. Can one seriously believe that Washington would have shrugged off such an attack on American lives and property as Japan delivered against the Philippines?

Nor were Japan's belligerent actions triggered by Hull's so-called ultimatum of November 26. [Japan's] Pearl Harbor [war] games of September 16, 1941, were predicated upon an X-Day of November 16. Only when it became evident that the task force could not be ready by that date was the attack postponed until December 7.

Prange hesitated to deal in absolutes, for he believed that the human equation was always subject to change without notice, but in the context of the time, he felt that war between Japan and the United States was virtually inevitable by late 1941, Pearl Harbor or no Pearl Harbor.

He also believed that one must consider the situation in the Atlantic, which could scarcely have been more explosive. Both Washington and Berlin had ignored incidents that gave at least technical excuse for declaring war. Almost certainly, sooner or later something would have happened that the United States or Germany would have found impossible to brush aside. If Roosevelt wanted war, he had no reason to push for it in the Pacific, especially in such an insane manner as encouraging the Japanese to hit Pearl Harbor.

Roosevelt's Dilemma

Roosevelt never pretended to be neutral in thought and paid only lip service to neutrality in deed. He sailed exceedingly close to the wind. Yet he knew that the United States was not ready militarily to take up the terrible burden to which history called it. Hence the apparent inconsistency of American actions in the late autumn of 1941. Perhaps no

President ever faced a more cruel dilemma than Roosevelt at that time. One may well believe that he felt an enormous release from tension when the Japanese took him off the hook. The entire timing of Pearl Harbor argued against the revisionist position. Throughout 1940 and 1941 U.S. diplomacy vis-à-vis Japan reflected a determined, almost frantic desire to buy time while the armed forces built up to the point where the country could become the "arsenal of democracy" and at the same time be able to resist Axis aggression in both theaters. On December 7, 1941, they still had a long way to go. Deliberately to bring about the very eventuality against which both Army and Navy had pleaded would have been the sheerest madness.

[Roosevelt] knew that the United States was not ready militarily to take up the terrible burden to which history called it.

What is more, Germany need not have invoked the Tripartite Pact when Japan struck the United States. The treaty called for Japan and Germany to come to each other's aid if attacked by a power not then in the war. Nothing was said about mutual aid if Germany, Japan, or Italy did the attacking. Japan used this loophole to escape joining its Axis partner in the Russo-German war, so why should Hitler feel any obligation toward the ally that had turned him down?

In his speech of December 8, 1941, asking Congress to declare "a state of war" with Japan, Roosevelt carefully avoided including Germany, although Stimson urged him to do so. The fact that Hitler decided upon war with the United States was probably less to honor the Tripartite Pact than a practical decision that the time was ripe. Otherwise, Hitler could have played a diplomatic masterstroke by disassociating himself from Japan's action. This would have given the United States and Great Britain precisely what they did not want—a war in Asia that would divide British strength and drain off American arms and supplies from the European front.

Churchill's Angle

Basic to the argument that Roosevelt wanted to haul the United States into war by way of Japan is the assumption that during much of 1941 the President had a secret agreement with Churchill that if Japan struck British territory, the United States would enter the conflict. Revisionists hold to this theory tenaciously despite evidence to the contrary.

Of course, the beleaguered British desired the United States as an active ally. But—and this is what the revisionists did not appear to understand—the British believed that a firm commitment from the United States in regard to the Far East would be the surest way of guaranteeing Japan's good behavior. Churchill yearned to see full American might brought to bear in the Atlantic. But preattack documents make it quite clear that he wanted Japan reined in lest it cut the British lifeline in the Indian Ocean. So he would have preferred American involvement in Europe without the British being plunged into a major war in the Far East. In a telegram to Roosevelt on May 15, 1940, he listed Britain's "immediate needs," which ended, "Sixthly, I am looking to you to keep that Japanese dog quiet in the Pacific. . . ."

By October 1940 matters had simmered down sufficiently for Churchill to risk reopening the Burma Road [a vital supply line to British colonies in Southeast Asia]. He asked Roosevelt if the President could send a large American squadron "to pay a friendly visit to Singapore. . . ." He explained, "I should be very grateful if you would consider action along these lines as it might play an important part in preventing the spreading of the war."

Churchill realized that a formal British-American alliance against Japan would entail certain risks. Japan might lower its head and charge instead of pulling in its horns. Nor did Churchill minimize the problems war with Japan would pose. But in his view, ". . . the entry of the United States into the war would overwhelm all evils put together." So Churchill, as positive a thinker as ever, looked for the silver lining, and was prepared to make the best of it regardless of which way the Japanese jumped.

The United States most urgently wanted to concentrate upon the Atlantic and avoid a confrontation with Japan.

There could be no question that most American hearts, as well as the national interests, pulled toward the white cliffs of Dover. And Roosevelt, backed by a majority of Congress, had bent neutrality far off center with the lend-lease arrangement. Therefore, the United States most urgently wanted to concentrate upon the Atlantic and avoid a confrontation with Japan. Stark's famous Plan DOG laid it on the line: "Any strength that we might send to the Far East would, by just so much, reduce the force of our blows against Germany and Italy."

Secret Agreement

Greaves asserted, "Early in 1941 administration officials reached a secret agreement with British and Dutch officials, which committed us to go to war against Japan if Japanese forces crossed a certain line." It so happened that representatives of the U.S. and British Army and Navy staffs held discussions in Washington from January 29 to March 27, 1941. These discussions culminated in a secret military agreement (ABC-1 of March 1941). "Roosevelt did not approve ABC-1, but the United States later amended Rainbow Five (its major war plan) to fit this strategy. Attempts were made at Singapore in April 1941 to work out an American-British-Dutch operating plan for the Pacific which set forth certain Japanese actions, which failure to counteract would place the signatories at a military disadvantage." Doubtless this is the "secret agreement" to which Greaves referred. However, both Marshall and Stark withheld approval because, among other reasons, ABC contained "political matters" and the proposals set forth did not constitute "a practical operating plan." These plans and discussions did not commit the United States politically to go to war with Japan, Germany, or both; they outlined the military strategy to be followed if the country joined the conflict.

The transferring of ships from the Pacific to the Atlantic and the institution of patrols in that ocean strained neutrality. Still, all this de facto support fell short of a formal alliance. Never famous for consistency, Roosevelt could have called a halt should circumstances appear so to dictate.

The famous meeting between Roosevelt and Churchill in Argentia Bay is a favorite target of revisionists. Barnes entertained no doubt that at Argentia Roosevelt and Churchill "arranged the details of entering the second World War through the backdoor, of a war with Japan." Actually Churchill's prime consideration in the Pacific was not to spread the war but to contain it. He feared that the Japanese

Navy might cut Britain's lifeline to the Commonwealth. And he believed that only a firm declaration of mutual commitment by the United States, the British Empire, the Netherlands, and perhaps the Soviet Union would restrain Japan.

For all of Roosevelt's sympathy with the British, at Argentia he knew that the time was not ripe for a promise to threaten Japan with war for the sake of a third party. All moral considerations aside, he held a very poor hand. The United States was militarily unprepared to challenge Japan and in short order might be in even worse shape. In a few days the [military] draft extension would come before the House of Representatives. If Congress scuttled the draft, the United States would not have enough of an army to defend itself, let alone help anyone else. What actually happened as a result of Argentia was that Roosevelt presented to Nomura a note promising to take "any and all steps which it may deem necessary" to safeguard the rights of American nationals and the security of the nation. It contained no word about American action in the event the Japanese attacked British or Dutch territory.

Assuring the British

Matters took a sharp turn on December 1, when Roosevelt met with Harry Hopkins and British Ambassador Lord Halifax. He thought the time had come for London and Washington to "settle what they would do in the various situations which might arise." If Japan attacked the British or Dutch, they "should obviously be all together. . . ." But to clear up certain matters "which were less plain," he wanted Halifax to ask for his government's policies in various eventualities.

Halifax already had instructions to tell the United States government that the British expected the Japanese to hit Thailand. Such an attack probably would include "a seaborne expedition to seize strategic points in the Kra Isthmus." The British "proposed to counter this . . . by a rapid move by sea into the Isthmus" to hold a line just north of Singone. But because of the dangerous political disadvantages should the Japanese beat the British to the punch, London "wanted to know urgently what view the United States Government would take of this plan, since it was most important for us to be sure of American support in the event of war."

Roosevelt assured the ambassador that his country "could certainly count on American support, though it might take a few days before it was given." On December 2 Churchill informed Foreign Minister Anthony Eden by memorandum:

> If the United States declares war on Japan, we follow within the hour. If, after a reasonable interval, the United States is found to be incapable of taking any decisive action, even with our immediate support, we will, nevertheless, although alone, make common cause with the Dutch.

Thus Churchill pledged support to the United States in much less equivocal terms than those Roosevelt used to Halifax.

Despite all these developments, Churchill and his government could not be certain that American "support" in Southeast Asia would mean that the United States would enter the European war. Hitler had only to keep his brown shirt on, and Great Britain might find itself with war on another front, assured of American "support" but not necessarily armed participation, and with the United States still out of the major conflict in Europe.

On the evening of December 3 Roosevelt informed Halifax that the British could count on "armed support." But the British understood that he still clung to a faint hope that he might work out a temporary truce with Japan through his personal approach to the Emperor.

So, after dodging the issue all year, on December 1 Roosevelt promised the British support in the Far East, and on December 3 armed support. The reason was clear: The problem was no longer one of restraining the Japanese; they were on the move. The only question was exactly where they would strike first. Of course, Roosevelt could not commit the United States to war with Japan on behalf of the British, the Dutch, the Thais, or anyone else. For this he would need congressional authority. "Armed support" for the British did not automatically involve going to war on their behalf; the United States had been giving Britain "armed support" against Hitler for months [via lend-lease] while technically clinging to neutrality.

In any case, the President's somewhat equivocal commitment came much too late to have any relationship to the Pearl

Harbor attack. Throughout 1941, while Roosevelt hesitated and the British fretted, the Japanese planned and trained for Operation Hawaii. By December 5 Nagumo had received orders to "Climb Mount Niitaka" and his ships' prows were irrevocably headed eastward. [Commander Mitsumi] Shimizu's submarines were lurking in Hawaiian waters. Above all, neither Yamamoto nor the Naval General Staff was considering Roosevelt's preferences. The Japanese based their naval strategy upon the foreign policy of one country and one only—Japan. . . .

Revisionists such as Barnes and Theobald believed their tissue of unsupported assumptions and assertions. By the same token, those who cannot swallow their thesis are not necessarily blind adulators of Roosevelt. The President made his mistakes in 1941, as did almost everyone else involved in Pearl Harbor. But in a thorough search of more than thirty years, including all publications released up to May 1, 1981, we have not discovered one document or one word of sworn testimony that substantiates the revisionist position on Roosevelt and Pearl Harbor.

Important Figures in the Attack on Pearl Harbor

Bloch, Claude C., Commander, Fourteenth Naval District, Honolulu

Bratton, Rufus S., Chief, Far Eastern Section, Army Intelligence (G2)

Fielder, Kendall, Chief U.S. Army Intelligence Officer, Hawaiian Department

Fuchida, Mitsuo, Commander, Air Groups, Japanese First Air Fleet

Hart, Thomas, Commander in Chief, U.S. Asiatic Fleet

Hull, Cordell, Secretary of State

Kimmel, Husband E., Commander in Chief, U.S. Pacific Fleet

Knox, Frank, Secretary of the Navy

Layton, Edwin T., Chief Intelligence Officer, U.S. Pacific Fleet

MacArthur, Douglas, Commanding General, U.S. Army Far East

Marshall, George C., Chief of Staff, U.S. Army

McCollum, Arthur H., Chief, Far Eastern Section, Office of Naval Intelligence

Miles, Sherman, Chief of Intelligence (G2), U.S. Army

Nagumo, Chuichi, Commander, Japanese First Air Fleet

Nomura, Kichisaburo, Japanese Ambassador to the United States

Roberts, Owen, Associate Supreme Court Justice and Roberts Commission Chairman

Roosevelt, Franklin D., President of the United States

Short, Walter C., Commanding General, Hawaiian Department, U.S. Army

Stark, Harold R., Chief of Naval Operations

Stimson, Henry L., Secretary of War

Tojo, Hideki, Prime Minister of Japan

Turner, Richmond Kelly, Commander, U.S. Navy War Plans Division

Wilkinson, Theodore Stark, Chief of Intelligence Division, Naval Operations

Yamamoto, Isoruko, Commander, Japanese Combined Fleet

Glossary

Army Pearl Harbor Board An official inquiry into the Pearl Harbor attack, convened in 1944 by the U.S. Army, which faulted General Short as well as General George C. Marshall for miscommunication and unpreparedness.

B-17 A high-level bomber, nicknamed the Flying Fortress, used by the U.S. Army during World War II.

Battleship Row The anchorage for U.S. battleships within Pearl Harbor, lying just east of Ford Island.

"Bomb Plot" message An intercepted message of October 9, 1941, in which Japan instructed its consulate in Hawaii to transmit a daily grid of U.S. Navy ship locations in Pearl Harbor and to log arrivals and departures of navy ships.

Dorn Report An inquiry into responsibility for the Pearl Harbor attack conducted by the undersecretary of defense, Edwin Dorn, in 1995.

dry dock A structure that allows engineers to expose a ship bottom free of water for repairs.

"East Wind Rain" message An intercepted "winds" message of December 3, 1941, in which Japan indicated a forthcoming break in diplomatic relations with the United States.

Ford Island An island lying in the middle of Pearl Harbor, used as an air base and naval station.

Fort Shafter U.S. Army Headquarters, Hawaiian Department, located on the island of Oahu.

"Fourteen Part" message An intercepted message sent by Japan to its ambassador in Washington on December 6, 1941, advising Japanese diplomats to destroy their code machines and papers and to deliver a declaration breaking diplomatic relations to the U.S. secretary of state the following afternoon (early morning in Pearl Harbor).

Hickam Field A U.S. Army Air Force base on Oahu, located just southeast of Pearl Harbor.

Joint Congressional Committee (JCC) hearings An official inquiry into the Pearl Harbor attack conducted by the U.S. Congress from November 18, 1945, until May 31, 1946.

Kaneohe Naval Air Station A U.S. navy air base located on a peninsula along the northeastern coast of Oahu.

kido butai   The Japanese term for the Pearl Harbor striking force.

Knox Report   An inquiry into responsibility for and damage resulting from the Pearl Harbor attack, conducted by Secretary of the Navy Frank Knox in Hawaii in January 1946.

Naval Court of Inquiry   An official inquiry into the Pearl Harbor attack conducted by the U.S. Navy from July 24 to October 19, 1944.

nisei   American citizens of Japanese descent.

Office of Naval Intelligence (ONI)   The agency charged with intercepting, decoding, and delivering messages and intelligence of interest to the U.S. Navy.

Opana Point   A point lying on the northern shore of the island of Oahu and the location of a military radar station in December 1941.

PBY   A U.S. Navy aircraft nicknamed the Catalina or flying boat, capable of landing at sea or on land.

Purple/Magic   "Magic" refers to the entire spectrum of Japanese diplomatic and military codes, which were being constantly changed by the Japanese in an effort to frustrate foreign code breakers. "Purple" refers to the specific Magic code reserved for the highest-level diplomatic messages between Tokyo and its embassies abroad.

Radio Corporation of America (RCA)   A leading private U.S. radio and telegraph company.

Roberts Commission   An official inquiry into the Pearl Harbor attack chaired by associate Supreme Court justice Owen Roberts, convened in Pearl Harbor from December 18, 1941, until January 23, 1942.

SBD   A dive-bomber nicknamed the Dauntless, used by the U.S. Marines and Navy during World War II.

Station HYPO   The U.S. Navy intelligence and decrypting center at Pearl Harbor.

"War Warning" message   A message sent on November 27, 1941, by Washington to U.S. military commanders in the Philippines, warning of an imminent Japanese attack.

Wheeler Field   A U.S. Army Air Force base, located five miles northwest of Pearl Harbor.

"Winds Execute" message   An intercepted message of November 28, 1941, in which Japan advised its diplomats that one of three "weather" codes would indicate the breaking of diplomatic relations with England, the United States, or the Soviet Union, signifying an imminent attack.

Zero: The nickname used by the American military for the AGM2 and AGM3 fighter planes used by Japan during World War II.

For Further Research

Books

Leonard Baker, *Roosevelt and Pearl Harbor.* New York: Macmillan, 1970.

Harry Barnes, *Pearl Harbor After a Quarter of a Century.* New York: Arno, 1972.

Dorothy Borg and Shumpei Okamoto, eds., *Pearl Harbor as History: Japanese American Relations, 1931–1941.* New York: Columbia University Press, 1973.

Richard Collier, *The Road to Pearl Harbor—1941.* New York: Atheneum, 1981.

Hilary Conroy and Harry Wray, eds., *Pearl Harbor Re-Examined: Prologue to the Pacific War.* Honolulu: University of Hawaii Press, 1990.

A.A. Hoehling, *December 7, 1941: The Day the Admirals Slept Late.* New York: Kensington, 1991.

Akira Iriye, *Pearl Harbor and the Coming of the Pacific War: A Brief History with Documents and Essays.* Boston: Bedford/St. Martin's, 1999.

Lee B. Kennett, *For the Duration . . . : The United States Goes to War, Pearl Harober, 1942.* New York: Scribner, 1985.

Husband E. Kimmel, *Admiral Kimmel's Story.* Chicago: H. Regnery, 1955.

Larry Kimmett and Margaret Regis, *The Attack on Pearl Harbor: An Illustrated History.* Seattle: Navigator, 1991.

Walter Lord, *Day of Infamy.* New York: Ulverscroft Group, 1997.

Martin V. Melosi, *The Shadow of Pearl Harbor: Political Controversy over the Surprise Attack.* College Station: Texas A&M University Press, 1977.

Sid Moody, *Pearl Harbor: Fiftieth Anniversary Special Edition.* Stamford, CT: Longmeadow, 1991.

Samuel Eliot Morison, *The Rising Sun in the Pacific, 1931–April, 1942.* Boston: Little, Brown, 1948.

Gordon W. Prange, *Pearl Harbor: The Verdict of History.* New York: McGraw-Hill, 1986.

Gordon W. Prange, wih Donald M. Goldstein and Katherine V. Dillon, *At Dawn We Slept: The Untold Story of Pearl Harbor.* New York: Penguin Books, 1982.

James Rusbridger and Eric Nave, *Betrayal at Pearl Harbor: How Churchill Lured Roosevelt into World War II.* New York: Summit Books, 1991.

Archie Satterfield, *The Day the War Began.* Westport, CT: Praeger, 1992.

Michael Slackman, *Target—Pearl Harbor*. Honolulu: University of Hawaii Press, 1990.

Robert A. Theobald, *The Final Secret of Pearl Harbor: The Washington Contribution to the Japanese Attack*. New York: Devin-Adair, 1954.

George M. Waller, ed., *Pearl Harbor: Roosevelt and the Coming of the War*. Lexington, MA: D.C. Heath, 1965.

Stanley Weintraub, *Long Day's Journey into War: December 7, 1941*. New York: Dutton, 1991.

Stephen Bower Young, *Trapped at Pearl Harbor: Escape from Battleship "Oklahoma."* Croton-on-Hudson, NY: North River, 1991.

Periodicals

Bruce Bartlett, "The Pearl Harbor Coverup," *Reason*, February 1976.

Hector Bywater, "The Great Pacific War," *Life*, December 22, 1941.

John Chamberlain, "The Man Who Pushed Pearl Harbor," *Life*, April 1, 1946.

Percy L. Greaves, "Pearl Harbor," *National Review*, December 13, 1966.

William H. Honan, "Japan Strikes: 1941," *American Heritage*, December 1970.

Sherman Miles, "Pearl Harbor in Retrospect," *Atlantic Monthly*, July 1948.

Samuel E. Morison, "Did Roosevelt Start the War: History Through a Beard," *Atlantic Monthly*, August 1948.

Videos

December 7th: The Movie. Directed by John Ford and Gregg Toland. Monterey, CA: Kit Parker Films, 1991.

Great Blunders of WWII. A & E Television Network. Distributed by New Video, 1998.

Pearl Harbor. Secrets of the Unknown series. Triumph Communications Production. MPI Home Video, 1989.

Pearl Harbor: Surprise and Remembrance. Presented by WGBH/Boston, WNET/New York, KCET/Los Angeles. Alexandria, VA: PBS Video, 1991.

Tora! Tora! Tora! An Elmo Williams–Richard Fleischer Production. Beverly Hills, CA: Fox Video, 1991.

Websites

Battleship Row: A Photographic Look at the U.S. Navy During the Attack on Pearl Harbor, December 7, 1941. www.geocities.com/CapeCanaveral/ Hangar/5515/.

Pearl Harbor Archive. www.sperry-marine.com/pearl/pearlh. htm.

Pearl Harbor Attack Hearings. www.ibiblio.org/pha/pha.

Pearl Harbor Remembered. www.execpc.com/~dschaaf/mainmenu. html.

Pearl Harbor Survivors' Association. http://members.aol.com/ phsasecy97/.

USS *Arizona* Memorial. www.nps.gov/usar/.

Index

125